HORSE SENSE

Pure & Simple

TEXAS BIX BENDER
author of *Don't Squat with Yer Spurs On!*

GIBBS·SMITH
P
PUBLISHER

SALT LAKE CITY

First Edition
06 05 04 03   *5 4 3*

Copyright © 1999 by Texas Bix Bender

Published by
Gibbs Smith Publisher
P.O. Box 667
Layton, Utah 84041
Web site: www.gibbs-smith.com

Library of Congress Cataloging-in-Publication Data
Bender, Texas Bix, 1949–
Horse sense : pure & simple / Texas Bix Bender.
p. cm.
ISBN 0-87905-886-2
1. Horses—Humor. 2. Conduct of life—Humor.
I. Title.
PN6231.H59 B46   1999
818'.5402—dc21   *98-46278*
                    CIP

STRAIGHT TALK RIGHT FROM THE HORSE'S MOUTH

by Piebald Plato
as told to Texas Bix Bender

Piebald Plato was a real horse. We had a lot of conversations together. Anybody who's ever been close to an animal knows they're not all that dumb. They can have a lot to say. Animals speak with their ears, their tails, their eyes, their noses, their posture, and sometimes with their mouths. Sometimes they say a lot by saying nothing at all.

Piebald was two years old when he came to be my friend. He was seventeen when lightning struck him and he went off to wherever we go when our number's up. In the meantime, I grew wiser for knowing him. This book is a distillation of what I learned from Piebald and a few other wise old nags.

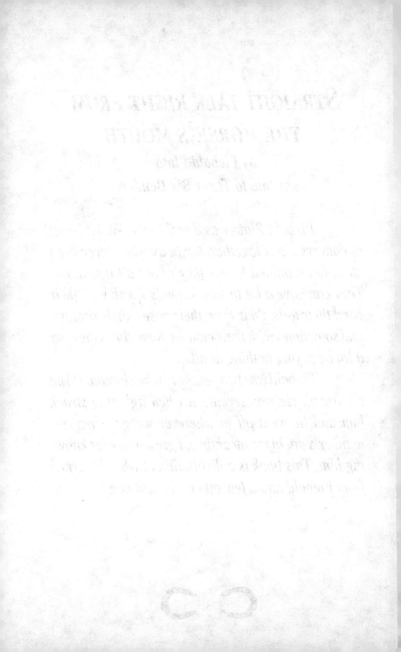

First came man,
then woman,
or something like that.
Either way,
if they wanted to ride,
they needed a horse,
so then came the horse.

*Take life
with a lick of salt.*

If you look a gift horse
in the mouth,
you could lose
a nose.

A horse
by any other name
would still be a horse.
Same goes
for a jackass.

*There's nothin' like
a good long walk,
especially if it's taken
by somebody you'd
like to get rid of.*

*Automobiles
should be shot
when they break down.*

*A lot of
clothes horses
oughta be shot.*

*If life is goin' by too fast,
try slowin' down
a bit on the turns.*

For every mile
of bad road you travel,
there're two miles of ditch
you're stayin' out of.

*Never cut
what you
can untie.*

*If you're hell-bent
for leather,
you'll get
where you're goin'.*

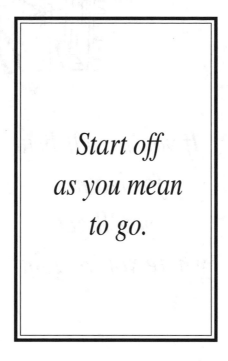

*Start off
as you mean
to go.*

*It is not possible
to run from something
you are tied to.*

*If you
stick your head
in the sand,
you can expect
a kick in the tail.*

Many are called
but few get up.

*You miss a lot
when you travel
at a gallop.*

*You don't have
to see the light
to feel the heat.*

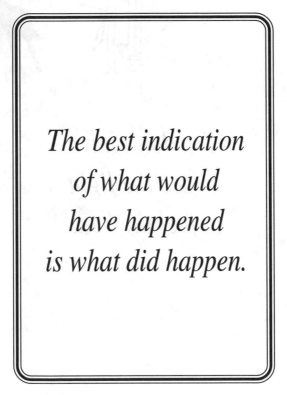

The best indication of what would have happened is what did happen.

Pint-size ponies
like to snort and stomp
just as much as big ones.

*The water won't clear up
until you get the hogs
outta the creek.*

You can't shoe
a running horse.

*A lot of mud holes
are deeper
than they look.*

*Better from the
horse's mouth
than a
horse's behind.*

*Have confidence
in your seat and
you will not lose it.*

*Crap not only happens,
it makes things grow.*

*A wild horse
has more secrets
than a gentle one.*

You can't judge a horse by its color. A bad horse is often a good color.

*Passing judgment
is not a good
course to pass.*

*Every jackass thinks
he's got horse sense.*

Finding a worm in your apple is a lot better than finding half a worm in your apple.

*People shouldn't
go around actin'
like any part of a horse.*

*Waitin' is easy
if your foot's
not the one
needin' a shoe.*

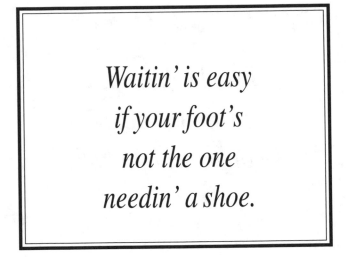

Frustration
is having a stump tail
in fly season.

*A night of
sowing wild oats
makes for
a poor breakfast.*

*There are
no friendly rattlers.*

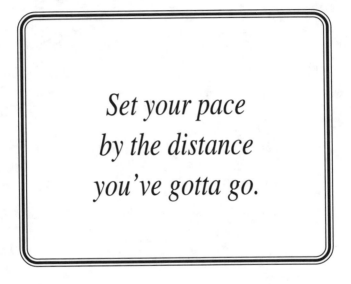

*Set your pace
by the distance
you've gotta go.*

*It takes more
than a pat on the back
to cure saddle sores.*

Pullin' somethin' up
by its roots
won't help it grow.

*If you stick your nose
into trouble, your feet
are bound to follow.*

*The farther
you run away,
the farther
it is back.*

44

The number of
traffic accidents
that happen every year
pretty much proves that
most of the horse sense
in the horse-and-buggy days
belonged to the horse.

*Nobody ever asks
how many miles
a horse gets
to a bale of hay.*

If fifty thousand people
ran daily at a racetrack,
not one horse
would come to watch.

The big difference between animals and humans is that animals have a healthier sex life.

*Things have a way
of workin' out
if you can just
keep your head
out of your behind.*

Life is relative.
If a raccoon picks a lock,
he gets featured on Nature.
If a man does it,
he gets three to five
in the hoosegow.

*If you've ever wondered
what horse feed tastes like,
eat a handful of unsalted
baked tortilla chips.*

When you tie on the feed bag,
be content with
a genteel sufficiency.
Any more than that
is a vulgar plenty.

A gentle horse
is soon curried.

*If you cross a bridge
before you get to it,
you pay the toll twice.*

You can't put a mirror
on the table
and eat on
your good looks.

*If you want
to swim,
you've gotta go
where the water
is deep.*

Mistakes are lessons
to be learned.

Complaining has about as much effect as the barking of a faraway dog.

*The best way out
is usually to
go on through.*

When you're runnin'
from somethin',
it's still good to know
where you're goin'.

The more you've got,
the more what you've got
has got you.

*What is natural
and what is right
make pretty good ground
to stand on.*

*If it's too much
to love your enemy,
then compromise and
just forget the knothead.*

*If you parley with
the wrong side,
you'll never get on
the right side.*

Many are cold,
but few are frozen.

*You can lead
a fool to talk,
but you can't make
him think.*

You can't convince a rooster
he doesn't know as much
about singin'
as a mockingbird.

*You have to love
a woman to know her—
even then,
there's a lot of
guesswork involved.*

Each day is a link
in a mighty long chain.

*It's better
to tell the truth and run
than to lie and
get caught.*

For thousands of years
coyotes have howled
at the moon . . .
still no answer.

Nothing is more
than half as
good as it would be
if it was twice
as good as it is.
On the other hand,
everything is twice as
good as it would be,
if it were only half
as good as it is.

*A fast horse
cannot go fast
far.*

Don't do nothin'
too much.

*The smoother the gab,
the smoother the dose.
You don't know you've been
had 'til you've swallowed it.*

The gobbler doesn't spread his tail feathers when his head's on the block.

The most successful liar
is the one
who doesn't do it
too often.

*The more promises
you make today,
the more excuses
you make
tomorrow.*

Life is now, and then.
Tomorrow is never.

*Better to have
a good hold
than a good place
to fall.*

*Swallow what you're chewin'
before you take
the next bite.*

*The saddle don't make
the horse.*

Let the wind do your sighing
and the clouds
cry your tears.

If tombstones told the truth,
hell would have
gone out of business
long ago.

The smile and
the rainbow
whisper hope.

*A comfortable ride
is what's best
for pony and rider.*

Short stirrups
make for a bad ride

It's not the sharpest spurs that do the most damage.

*If you want to
work up to
bein' a good rider,
you've got
some mud to eat.*

*An unsaddled pony
will often show
no vice at all,
but when ridden
and fed
he may display
all manner of sin.*

*A pony that
shies and rears
is unsafe in traffic.*

You can't insult arrogance.

When given a choice,
a critter will always head
for the wrong gate.

Two's a coincidence,
three's an outbreak.

*There is art
even in the cleaning
of a stable.*

*If it's your
behind that's itchin',
it won't do any good
to scratch your head.*

*If you want a horse
to know you,
breathe up its nose
the first time you meet.*

When the horse
is spent,
a stronger whip
won't refresh him.

98

*A young pony
is quick to pick up
an old horse's
bad habits.*

About half a mind to do something usually gets it about half done.

The bigger the spur,
the bigger the prick.

Horses can't speak English, but they do speak fluent Horse.

*"Forked down" is
landing on your head
with your rusty dusty
up in the air. "Fork end up" is
landing on your sit-down
with your legs up in the air.
Just plain "forked"
means it's over—
there's nothing up in the air.*

Conform and be dull.

When the bull is loose . . .
no sudden moves.

*A good friend
makes every mile
you travel together
a little shorter.*

A horse is still a horse
without a rider,
but a rider without a horse
is afoot.

What you can't jump,
you gotta go around.

*If you have nothing to do,
don't do it.*

*Drownin' your
sorrows seldom works,
as most of 'em
can swim.*

Too much ain't healthy.

*A stampede
has no conscience.*

Shallow streams
and shallow minds
freeze first.

It's easier
to catch a horse
than ride one.

*You have to
control yourself
before you can
control your horse.*

*The only way
to a clean stable
is to get dirty.*

*A blind horse
sees just as well
from either end.*

*Never spur a horse
when he's swimmin'.*

Lightning does the work;
thunder takes the credit.

*If you
throw your loop
half a dozen times
and miss your mark,
the only thing to do
is lie about it.*

When in doubt,
let your horse
do the thinkin'.

*Not makin' a choice
is makin' a choice.*

Everybody's a rider
on a gentle horse.

*An old horse for
a long hard road,
a young pony for
a quick ride.*

*Every horse looks tall
in a short herd.*

*It does no good
to sell your horse
to buy a saddle.*

Given
8/17/97 by
Shelly Na.

THE
LIMITLESS
love
OF
CHRIST

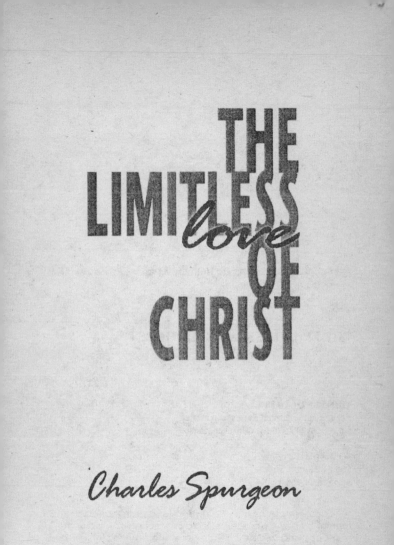

THE LIMITLESS *love* OF CHRIST

Charles Spurgeon

Whitaker House

All Scripture quotations are from the *King James Version* (KJV) of the Bible.

THE LIMITLESS LOVE OF CHRIST

ISBN: 0-88368-458-6
Printed in the United States of America
Copyright © 1996 by Whitaker House

Whitaker House
580 Pittsburgh Street
Springdale, PA 15144

1 2 3 4 5 6 7 8 9 10 11 / 06 05 04 03 02 01 00 99 98 97 96

Contents

1. Oh, How He Loves!... 7

2. Love's Birth and Parentage 29

3. A Blessed Gospel Chain............................... 59

4. God's Love for the Saints............................ 89

5. Love at Leisure 113

6. Unparalleled Lovingkindnesses................ 139

1

Oh, How He Loves!

*Then said the Jews,
Behold how he loved him!
—John 11:36*

It was at the grave of Lazarus that Jesus wept, and His grief was so manifest to the onlookers that they said, *"Behold how he loved him!"* I trust that most of us, however, are not mere onlookers, but we share in the special love of Jesus. We see evidences of that love, not in His tears, but in the precious blood that He so freely shed for us.

We ought to marvel even more than those Jews did at the love of Jesus, see further into His heart than they did, and know more of

7

Him than they could in the brief interval in which they knew Him. When we think of His love for us, we may well cry, "Behold how He has loved us!" The Jews expressed their wonder at the love that Jesus had for His friend Lazarus. They did not keep that wonder to themselves, but they said, *"Behold how he loved him!"*

In these days we are too apt to repress our emotions. I cannot say that I greatly admire the way some enthusiastic people shout, "Glory!" "Hallelujah!" "Amen!" and so on in the midst of sermons and prayers. Yet, I would sooner have a measure of that enthusiastic noise than have you constantly stifling your natural emotions and checking yourself from expressing your heart's true feelings.

If we were in a right state of mind and heart, we would often say to one another, "How wondrous has the love of Jesus been to us!" Our conversation with one another, as fellow Christians, would often be on this subject. We waste far too much time upon trifles. It would be well if the love of Jesus so engrossed our thoughts that it engrossed our conversation, too.

I fear that many who profess to be Christians go for a whole year, or even longer, without telling others what they have experienced of the love of Jesus. This should not be the case. If we were as we should be, one would frequently say to another, "How great is Christ's love for me, my friend! Is it the same for you?" Such talk between the saints on earth would help us anticipate the time when we will want to talk about nothing else.

I am going to remind you of some very simple truths in order to excite your heart toward our Lord and Savior, who has loved you so intensely that He died for you. First, we will consider what the love of Christ has done for us; secondly, what His love has done to us; and then, thirdly, I want to encourage you to develop and maintain a strong, noticeable response of love for Christ.

What Christ's Love Has Done for Us

So, first, let us think over what the love of Christ has done for us.

When did Christ's love begin to work for us? It was long before we were born, long before the world was created. Far, far back in eternity, our Savior gave the first proof of His love to us by espousing our cause. By His divine foresight, He looked upon human nature as a palace that had been plundered and broken down, and in its ruins He perceived all manner of unclean things. Who was there to undertake the great work of restoring that ruined palace? No one but the Word, who was with God, and who was God (John 1:1).

> *He saw that there was no man, and won-*
> *dered that there was no intercessor: there-*
> *fore his arm brought salvation unto him;*
> *and his righteousness, it sustained him.*
> *(Isa. 59:16)*

He Espoused Our Cause

Before the angels began to sing or the sun and moon and stars threw their first beams across primeval darkness, Christ espoused the cause of His people. He resolved not only to restore all the blessings that they would eventually lose, but also to add to them richer favors than could ever have been theirs except through Him.

Even from eternity His delights were with the sons of men. In that far distant past, which we can hardly imagine, Christ became *"the head over all things to the church"* (Eph. 1:22), which then existed only in the mind of God. When I think of this, my very soul cries out in a rapture of delight, "Behold how He loved us!"

He Became Our Representative

Remember, too, that in that eternal secret council, the Lord Jesus Christ became the Representative and Surety of His chosen people. There was to be, in what was then the far remote future, a covenant between God and man. But, who was there who was both able and willing to sign that covenant on man's behalf? Who would guarantee that man's part of that covenant would be fulfilled?

It was then that the Son of God, well knowing all that such a covenant would involve, offered to be the Surety for His people. He pledged to fulfill the covenant on their behalf and to meet every one of its demands that He foresaw them unable to meet. Then the eternal Father gave into Christ's charge the souls that He had chosen for eternal life, though many ages were to elapse before these souls were to be created. The eternal Son covenanted to redeem all these souls after they had fallen through sin, to keep them by His grace, and to present them *"faultless before the presence of his* [Father] *with exceeding joy"* (Jude 1:24).

Thus, as Jacob became accountable to Laban for the whole flock committed to his charge, Jesus Christ, *"that great shepherd of the sheep, through the blood of the everlasting covenant"* (Heb. 13:20), undertook to redeem and guard the whole flock entrusted to His care. The blessed Shepherd-Son, therefore, at the last great muster, should be able to say to His Father as they pass under His hand, *"Those that thou gavest me I have kept, and none of them is lost"* (John 17:12).

It was in the everlasting covenant that our Lord Jesus Christ became our Representative and Surety and engaged on our behalf to fulfill all of His Father's will. As we think of this great mystery of mercy, surely all of us who are truly His must exclaim with grateful adoration, "Behold how He loved us!"

He Took on Our Nature

I have been writing of very ancient things so far, but now we come to matters that we can more clearly comprehend. In the fullness of time, our Lord Jesus Christ left the glories of heaven and took upon Himself our human nature. We know so little of what the word "heaven" means that we cannot adequately appreciate the tremendous sacrifice that the Son of God made in order to become the son of Mary. The holy angels could understand far better than we can what Christ gave up when He renounced the royalties of heaven and left

His throne and crown above, to be born as the babe of an earthly mother. All the honor and glory that rightly belonged to Him as the Son of the Highest were put aside.

Yet, even the angels could not fathom all the mysteries about His incarnation. As they followed the footprints of the Son of Man on His way from the manger to the cross to the tomb, they must often have been in that attitude of which Peter wrote, *"which things the angels desire to look into"* (1 Pet. 1:12).

To us, the incarnation of Christ is one of the greatest marvels in the history of the universe, and we say, as Paul did, *"Without controversy great is the mystery of godliness: God was manifest in the flesh"* (1 Tim. 3:16). The omnipotent Creator took the nature of a creature into indissoluble union with His divine nature; and, marvel of marvels, that creature was man. *"He took not on him the nature of angels; but he took on him the seed of Abraham"* (Heb. 2:16).

If it were possible for an angel to become an ant, it would be nothing at all in comparison with the condescension of Christ in becoming the babe of Bethlehem. After all, angels and ants are only creatures formed by Christ, as John, writing under the inspiration of the Holy Spirit, expressly said, *"All things were made by him; and without him was not any-thing made that was made"* (John 1:3).

There was never any other love like our Savior's. That the eternal Son of God would leave His Father's side and stoop so low as to become one with His chosen people—so that Paul could truly have written, *"We are members of his body, of his flesh, and of his bones"* (Eph. 5:30)—is such a wonder of condescending grace and mercy that we can only exclaim again and again, "Behold how He loved us!"

He Endured Our Infirmities

Then, *"being found in fashion as a man"* (Phil. 2:8), He took upon Himself human sickness and suffering. All our infirmities that were not sinful, Jesus Christ endured—the weary feet, the aching head, and the palpitating heart—

> *that it might be fulfilled which was spoken by Esaias the prophet, saying, Himself took our infirmities, and bare our sicknesses.*
> *(Matt. 8:17)*

This was a wondrous proof of love: the Son of God, who did not need to suffer, was willing to suffer infirmity just like any other man.

We have not an high priest which cannot be touched with the feeling of our infirmities; but was in all points tempted like as we are, yet without sin. (Heb. 4:15)

If you want to see the love of Jesus at the highest point it ever reached, you must, by faith, gaze upon Him when He took the sins of all His people upon Himself. Peter wrote of Christ, *"who his own self bare our sins in his own body on the tree"* (1 Pet. 2:24). How could one who was so pure, so absolutely perfect, ever bear so foul a load? Yet, He did bear it, and the transfer of His people's sin to Him was so complete that the inspired prophet wrote, *"The LORD hath laid on him the iniquity of us all"* (Isa. 53:6). The inspired apostle, likewise, wrote, *"He hath made him to be sin for us, who knew no sin; that we might be made the righteousness of God in him"* (2 Cor. 5:21).

When a man marries a woman who is deeply in debt, knowing full well that the burden he is taking upon himself might be enough to crush him all his life, we might say, "Behold how he loves her!" That was what Christ did for His church when He took her into an eternal marriage union with Himself, although all of her debts could not have been excused if she spent eternity in hell. He took all her debts upon Himself, and then He paid them unto the *"uttermost farthing"* (Matt. 5:26).

We must never forget that when Christ bore His people's sins, He also bore the full punishment of them. In fulfillment of the great eternal covenant, and in prospect of all the glory and blessing that would follow from Christ's atoning sacrifice, *"it pleased the LORD to bruise him; he hath put him to grief"* (Isa. 53:10).

We cannot have the slightest conception of what that bruising and that grief were like. We do not know what our Lord's physical and mental agonies must have been, yet they were only the shell of His sufferings. How could we know? His soul was agonized when God turned His face away from Him for the first time. It was that which made Him cry, *"My God, my God, why hast thou forsaken me?"* (Matt. 27:46).

It was then that the precious *"corn of wheat"* fell into the ground and died; and dying, it brought forth *"much fruit"* (John 12:24), of which heaven and eternity alone can tell the full tale. Words seem to limit me when I write of this wondrous mystery, and I cannot seem to write it clearly enough, but if you know even in part what it means, then join me by saying, "Behold how He loved us!"

All That He Has Is Ours

Further than that, Christ has so completely given Himself to us that all that He has is ours. He is the glorious husband, and His church is His bride, the Lamb's wife. There is nothing that He has that is not also hers even now and that He will not share with her forever. By a marriage bond that cannot be broken, for He *"hateth putting away"* (Mal. 2:16), He has joined with her in righteousness and truth. She will be one with Him throughout eternity. He has gone up to His Father's house to take possession of the many mansions there (John 14:2), not for Himself, but for His people. His constant prayer is,

Father, I will that they also, whom thou hast given me, be with me where I am; that they may behold my glory, which thou hast given me: for thou lovedst me before the foundation of the world.   *(John 17:24)*

Jesus has an ever-flowing fountain of joy in His heart, but if you belong to Him, He desires that His joy may be in you and that your joy may be full (John 16:24). Everything else that He has is yours as much as it is His, so join with me again by saying, "Behold how He loves us!"

What Christ's Love Has Done to Us

Now, secondly, let us consider what Christ's love has done to us, for each of His acts of love should cause us to exclaim, "Behold how He loves us!"

In the Past

Think back now on how the Lord dealt with us in the days of our unregeneracy. He called us again and again, but we would not go to Him. Oftentimes, the more lovingly He called us, the more we hardened our hearts and refused to accept His gracious invitation. With some of us, this refusal lasted for years, and we wonder now why the Lord waited so long for us.

If a rich man invites a pauper to a feast, and the poor man is indifferent to the invitation or positively refuses to accept it, he gets no second invitation, for the rich man does not press his charity upon the needy. On the other hand, when we scoffed at our Lord's call and made every excuse we could for not coming to the gospel banquet, He would not take our no for an answer. Instead, He called and called, again and again, until at last we could hold out no longer and had to yield to the sweet compulsion of His grace.

Oh, How He Loves!

Do you remember how you received pardon and justification and adoption and the indwelling of the Spirit? Do you recall how the many *"exceeding great and precious promises"* (2 Pet. 1:4) were brought to you, like the various courses at a royal festival, served upon golden dishes adorned with priceless gems? Recall that blessed day when you first came and sat among the guests at the great King's table! As you look back upon it, your heart glows in grateful remembrance of Christ's mercy to you, and you cannot help saying, "Behold how He loved us!"

In the Present

Many days have passed since then, and I ask you now to recollect what Christ has done with you since you first trusted in Him. Has His love for you cooled in the slightest degree? All of us have tested that love at one time or another by our wandering and waywardness, but we have not quenched it, and its fire still burns just as vehemently as at the first.

We have sometimes fallen so low that our hearts have been incapable of emotion; yet Jesus has loved us all the while, and He softens our hard hearts as the glorious sun melts the icebergs of the sea. We were like grass that refuses the dew, yet the dew of His love gently fell upon us; and though we had not sought it, our hearts were refreshed by it.

Our Lord has indeed proved how He loved us by the gracious way in which He bears with our many provocations. He has enriched us with an abundance of gifts, He has sustained us with many comforts, and He has renewed our failing strength with His divine energy.

Take a pencil and paper, and try to write down in words or numbers your total indebtedness to His love. Where will you begin? And when you have begun, where will you finish? If you were to record only one out of every million of His love-gifts to you, would the whole world be able to contain the volumes that might be written? No, all you can say is, "Behold how He has loved us!"

Yet, there is more to it than that. The King Himself has brought us into His banqueting house, and His banner over us has been love (Song 2:4). He has not only permitted us to sit at His feet, as Mary did, but He has allowed us to pillow our heads on His bosom, as John did. He has even let us put our fingers into the print of the nails. Our friendship with Him is so familiar that He is not ashamed to call us His own. Once again we must say, "Behold how He loves us!"

In the Future

I must, however, mention one more proof of Christ's love, and that is this: He has made us long for heaven and has given us at least a measure of preparation for it. One of these days, if the chariot and horses of fire (2 Kings 2:11) do not stop at our door, we are expecting that our dear Lord and Savior will fulfill His promise to us:

> *If I go and prepare a place for you, I will come again, and receive you unto myself; that where I am, there ye may be also.*
> *(John 14:3)*

To a true believer in Jesus, the thought of departing from this world and going to be forever with the Lord (1 Thess. 4:17), has no sadness or gloom associated with it whatsoever. This earth is the place of our banishment and exile; heaven is our home. We are like the loving wife who is parted by thousands of miles of sea and land from her dear husband, and we are longing for the great reunion with our beloved Lord, from whom we shall then never again be separated (Rom. 8:38–39).

I cannot hope to depict the scene when Jesus will introduce us to the principalities and powers in heavenly places. He will bid us sit with Him at His throne, even as He sits with God the Father at His throne. Surely, the holy angels, who have never sinned, will then unite in exclaiming, "Behold how He loves them!"

The thought that we may be up there before another hour has passed brings contentment to my mind. Nevertheless, it will not be long before all of us who love the Lord will be with Him where He is, and then the least among us will know more of His love than the greatest of us can ever know while here below. Meanwhile, we have much of the joy of heaven even while we are upon this earth, for, as Paul wrote to the Ephesians,

> *God, who is rich in mercy, for his great love wherewith he loved us, even when we were dead in sins, hath quickened us together with Christ, (by grace ye are saved;) and hath raised us up together, and made us sit together in heavenly places in Christ Jesus.* (Eph. 2:4–6)

Our Love for Him

The closing portion of this chapter is to be very practical. Did anybody ever say of you, "Behold how he loves Christ"? If someone did say this, was it true? I know your answer: "Oh, I do love Him! He knows all things, and He knows that I love Him." But, do you love Him so fervently that strangers or even your more intimate acquaintances would say of you what the Jews said of His love for Lazarus, *"Behold how he loved him"*? Do you wish you could love Him so? Then consider what some saints have done to show how they loved their Lord.

Suffering for Christ's Sake

If you have read *Foxe's Book of Martyrs*, you know how hundreds of brave men and women—and children, too—have suffered for Christ's sake. They have lain in damp dungeons and have refused to accept liberty at the price of treachery to their Lord and His truth. They have been stretched upon the rack, yet no torture could make them yield up their fidelity to God.

Many have stood at the stake, gloriously calm and often triumphantly happy, and were burned to death for Christ's sake. Many onlookers learned to imitate their noble example. Others, who heard their dying testimonies and their expiring songs (not groans), could not help exclaiming, "Behold how these martyrs love their Master!"

Sacrificial Service

There have been others who have shown their love for the Lord through untiring and self-sacrificing service. At times they have labored for Him amid many perils, some as missionaries in foreign lands and others with equal zeal in this country. They spent their time and strength in seeking to win souls for Christ, and their hearts were all aglow with love for Him, so that those who knew them could not help saying, "Behold how they love their Lord!" Some of us can never hope to wear the ruby crown of martyrdom, yet we may be honored by receiving the richly jeweled crown from the hand of Christ as He says to each of His true laborers, *"Well done, thou good and faithful servant...enter thou into the joy of thy Lord"* (Matt. 25:21).

Fervent Prayer for Sinners

Then, too, we have known some saints who showed their love for their Lord by weeping over sinners and praying for their conversion. There have been gracious men and women who could not sleep at night because of their concern for the eternal welfare of their relatives, friends, or even lost ones who were personally unknown to them. These saints

have risen from their beds to agonize in prayer
for sinners who were either calmly sleeping
and not even dreaming of their doom, or else at
that very hour were adding to their many previous transgressions.

There have been others who could not
hear a blasphemous word as they passed along
the street without feeling a holy indignation at
the injury being done to their Lord. At the
same time, their eyes filled with tears of pity
for the poor blasphemers, and their hearts
poured out a stream of supplication for those
who were thus ignorantly or wantonly sinning
against the Most High. They have been like
Jeremiah, weeping over the lost, and like
Moses and Paul, ready to sacrifice their own
souls for the sake of others, until men have
been compelled to say, "Behold how these
weeping and pleading saints love their Lord
and love lost sinners for His sake!"

Tithes and Offerings

Still others have proved their love for their
Lord by the way in which they have given of
their finances to His cause. They have not only
given a tithe of all they had to the great
Melchizedek (see Hebrews 7:1–4), but they
have counted it a high privilege to lay all that

they had upon His altar. They assert that their gold was never so golden as when it was all Christ's and that their lands were never so valuable to them as when they were gladly surrendered to Him.

Even today, there are so few who thus imitate their Lord, who freely gave Himself and all He had that He might save His people. The church would do well to return to th days when *all that believed were together, and had all things common; and sold their possessions and goods, and parted them to all men, as every man had need*" (Acts 2:44–45).

Smaller Matters

Another most admirable way of proving our love for Christ is by being scrupulously careful to please Him in little things as well as in the more important matters. One of the worst signs of this present evil age is that so little is thought of even the great things of Christ—His atoning sacrifice, His high priestly character and work, His kingly rule, and so on. Meanwhile, the little things of Christ, those that are less by comparison with these, are often utterly despised.

There was a time in Scotland when men of God signed the Solemn League and Covenant with their blood. How many would do that to-day? One jewel in Christ's crown, that priceless crown of the King of Kings, was sufficient to call into the battlefield the noblest of Scotland's sons. But, today, the very crown of Christ itself is kicked about like a football by some of His professed servants. They set up their own fallible judgments against His infallible revelation, and so they practically say, "We will not have this Man to reign over us!"

Our Puritan forefathers were so scrupulous that men called them straitlaced, sour-faced, bigoted, and I know not what else. Nowadays, many of the truths for which they contended are said to be unimportant or of no account whatsoever. The special truth that distinguishes us as followers of Christ is regarded by many with supreme contempt.

Not long ago, a professedly Christian minister told me that he did not care one bit about baptism. If he belongs to Christ, he will have to answer to his Master for that saying; but I could not utter such a sentence as that without putting my very soul in jeopardy. He who really loves his Lord will not trifle with the least jot or tittle of his Lord's will. Love is one of the most jealous things in the universe. *"God is a jealous God"* (Deut. 6:15) because *"God is love"* (1 John 4:8).

The wife who truly loves her husband will not harbor even a wanton imagination; her fidelity to him must not be stained by even one unchaste thought. So must it be with every true lover of the Lord Jesus Christ. God grant that we, beloved of Christ, may do our Lord's will so scrupulously—in great things, in little things, and in all things alike—that those who see us in our daily lives may be compelled to say, "Behold how these Christians love Jesus Christ, their Lord and Savior!"

Yet, we must remember that, when our love has reached its highest point, it can only be like a solitary dewdrop trembling on a leaf compared with the copious showers of love that pour continually from the heart of our dear Lord and Master. Put all our loves together, and they will not fill a tiny cup; yet there before us flows the fathomless, limitless, scoreless ocean of the love of Jesus. Still, let us have all the love for Him that we can.

May the Holy Spirit fill our souls to the brim with love for Jesus, for His dear name's sake! Amen.

2

Love's Birth and Parentage

We love him, because he first loved us.
—1 John 4:19

These are very simple words, but very full of meaning. I might say of this sentence what one poet has said of prayer: it is "the simplest form of speech that infant lips can try," and yet it is one of the "sublimest strains that reach the majesty on high." Ask a little believing child why she loves the Savior, and she will reply at once, "Because He loved me and died for me." Then ascend to heaven where the saints are *"perfect in Christ Jesus"*

(Col. 1:28) and ask the same question; with united breath the whole choir of the redeemed will reply, "He has *loved us and washed us from our sins in his own blood*'" (Rev. 1:5).

When we begin to love Christ, *"we love him, because he first loved us."* In our previous chapter, we saw what His love has done for us and what blessings we have received because of that love. I also listed some means by which we may demonstrate our love for Him in return. But, what is, in fact, the relationship between His love for us and our love for Him? Where does our love for Him originate? When we grow in grace (2 Pet. 3:18) until we are capable of the highest degree of spiritual understanding and affection, we still have no better cause for loving Him than *"because he first loved us."*

In regard to our text, I pray that you may first *feel* it. The difference between a text read or heard and a text felt within the soul is remarkable. Oh, that you may be able to say from your heart because you cannot help saying it, "I love Him." If you were to spend the next hour or so exercising the emotion of love for God instead of reading further, it would be time well spent. It is extremely beneficial to the soul to take her fill of the love of the Lord Jesus. The sweet cure for all her ailments is for her to have leisure to delight herself in the

Lord and faith enough to dwell at ease in His perfections. Be sure, then, to let your heart have room, scope, and opportunity for enkindling the sacred passion of love for God.

If the second part of the text, *"he first loved us,"* is made equally as vivid to you by the power of faith, your heart will be *"satisfied as with marrow and fatness"* (Ps. 63:5). If the love of God in Christ Jesus is shed abroad in your heart by the Holy Spirit (Rom. 5:5), you will need no sermons. Your inward experience will be better than any talk.

May your love, like a drop of dew, be exhaled and carried up into the boundless heaven of God's love. May your heart ascend to the place where your treasure is and rest itself upon the heart of God. You will be blessed if Christ's love and yours are both fully *known and felt* at this moment. Pray that the Spirit will cause it to be so. This will bring our text into action, and that is a thousand times better than the mere quiet letter.

If you have visited the art galleries at Versailles, where the historic wars of France are set forth in glowing colors upon the canvas, you must have been struck by the pictures and interested in the terrible scenes. Upstairs in the same palace, there is a vast collection of portraits. I have traversed those galleries of portraits without much interest, pausing only here and there to notice a remarkable countenance. Very few people linger there; everyone seems to walk on as quickly as the polished floors allow.

Now, why is it that you are interested in the paintings downstairs and not by those upstairs? They are the same people, very many of them in the same dress. Why do you not gaze upon them with interest? The reason lies in that a portrait in still life, as a rule, can never have the same attraction as a scene of stirring action. The warrior dealing a terrible blow with his battle ax or the senator delivering an oration in the assembly is more notable than the same bodies and faces in repose. Life is impressive; action awakens thought. It is just so with our passage of Scripture.

Look at it as a matter of doctrine: *"We love him, because he first loved us."* If you are a thoughtful person, you will consider it well. *Feel* the fact itself, feel the love of God, know it within your own soul, and manifest it in your life; then see how engrossing it becomes.

With this as an introduction, I intend to use the text for four purposes: first, for doctrinal instruction; then, for experimental information; thirdly, for practical direction; and fourthly, for argumentative defense.

Doctrinal Instruction

He First Loved Us

We will use the text briefly for doctrinal instruction, one point of which is very clear, namely, that God's love for His people is first. *"He first loved us."* Make sure you understand this, because forgetfulness about it breeds much error, and more ignorance. God's love for us precedes our love for Him.

According to Scripture, it must be first because it is eternal. The Lord chose His people in Christ Jesus from *"before the foundation of the world"* (Eph. 1:4). To each one of His people this text may be applied: *"Yea, I have loved you with an everlasting love"* (Jer. 31:3). From all eternity the Lord looked upon His people with an eye of love; and as nothing can be before eternity, His love was first.

Certainly He loved us before we had a being, for He gave His Son to die for us long, long before our infant cries had saluted our mothers' ears. He loved us before we had any desire to be loved by Him, even when we were provoking Him to His face and displaying the fierce enmity of our unrenewed hearts.

Remember this: *"His great love wherewith he loved us, even when we were dead in sin"*

33

(Eph. 2:4–5). *"God commendeth His love toward us, in that, while we were yet sinners, Christ died for us"* (Rom. 5:8). When we did not have even a single throb of spiritual feeling, one pulse of hope, or one breath of desire, the Lord loved us even then.

The love of God is before our seeking; He draws us before we run after Him. We do not seek that love; that love seeks us. We wander further and further from it, resist it, and prove ourselves unworthy of it. Our nature offers nothing congenial to divine love, but the love of God arises in its freeness and stays us by its power over the conscience and the will. *"Ye have not chosen me, but I have chosen you"* (John 15:16) is the voice of sovereign grace. Let our response be: *"By the grace of God* [we are] *what* [we are]" (1 Cor. 15:10).

The Lord's love is before any repentance on our part. Impenitent sinners would never repent if God did not love them first. The Lord hates sin, yet He compassionately loved us when sin was pleasant to us, when neither the thunders of His law nor the wooings of His Gospel could persuade us to turn from it. When our hearts felt no convictions of sin and when there was no regret because of offenses against a gracious God, He loved us even then. What a gracious and loving God we have!

We, as Christians, are possessors of faith in Jesus Christ, but our faith did not come before His love. On the contrary, our faith rests in what that love has done for us of old. When we were unbelieving and hard-hearted, when we resisted the testimony of the Holy Spirit and put from us the word of eternal life, even then the Lord pitied us. Even then He had mercy upon us and continued to invite, to entreat, to persuade, until at last we believed and entered into a sense of His love.

There might be much about you now that God divinely approves, but these things were not there at first. They did not precede divine love, but they are the fruits of it. To use an old English word that has lost some of its original meaning, the love of God is a *preventing* love— it goes before any right motives of the soul and chronologically precedes any desires, wishes, aspirations, or prayers on our part.

Are you devout? God's love came before your devotion, for originally you were not so. Are you holy? Your holiness follows upon His love, for He loved you when you were unholy. He chose you that you might become more like Him by the sanctifying influences of His Spirit, and He loves His image in you.

Nevertheless, He loved you when that image was not there. He looked upon you with

35

infinite compassion when the image of the Devil was evident both in your character and your nature. However early in life you began to love the Lord, His love was first.

Our human nature provides no basis for the love of God being directed toward us. God loved us because He wished to love us, or, as our Lord put it, *"Even so, Father: for so it seemed good in your sight"* (Matt. 11:26). He had reasons in His own nature, good reasons, brought forth from the best conceivable place, namely, from His own perfections.

However, He has not entirely communicated those reasons to us. He tells us that He will have mercy on whom He will have mercy, and will have compassion on whom He will have compassion (Rom. 9:15). Thus He tries the submissiveness of our hearts, and we must bow in reverent silence to His righteous will.

Divine love is its own cause and does not follow from anything in us whatsoever. It flows spontaneously from the heart of God. This is a great comfort to us because, being uncreated, that love is unchangeable. If it had been set upon us because of some goodness in us, then, when the goodness was diminished, the love would diminish, too.

If God had loved us second and not first, or had the cause of the love been in us, that cause might have altered; the supposed effect, His love, would have altered, too. But now, whatever the believer's condition may be today, and however he may have wandered, the Lord declares, *"I do earnestly remember him still"* (Jer. 31:20).

God cannot have loved us first for any sinlessness on our part. He foreknew all the sin you ever would have; it was all present before His mind. Yet He loved you, and He still loves you. *"I am the LORD, I change not; therefore ye sons of Jacob are not consumed"* (Mal. 3:6). Since He is first, let us give Him the first place in our thoughts, the highest throne in our hearts, the royal position in our souls. Glorify Him, for He is first!

God's Love Causes Ours

Another part of the doctrine of the text is this: the love of God is the *cause* of our love for God. One thing may be first and another second, and yet the first might not be the cause of the second. There might not be any actual link between the two. To say, *"We love him, because he first loved us,"* signifies not only that we consciously love with this motive, but it also reminds us that this is the divine power that created that love in us.

Would we have loved God if He had not first given His Son to die for us? Had there been no redeeming sacrifice, would we have had any love for God? Unredeemed men, left to go on like fallen angels in their sin, would have had no more love for God than fallen angels have. How could they? Yet the Son, given to redeem, is the great foundation of love. God gives His Son, reveals His own love, and creates ours. When we remember Calvary, do we not see His love as the cause of ours?

But, imagine that you have never heard of Calvary. God might have given His Son to die for men; yet because you were not aware of it, you did not love Him. It is no small grace on God's part that *"to you is the word of this salvation sent"* (Acts 13:26). The heathen have never heard the message of salvation, but by His gracious providence you have been favored with the Good News. You have it in your home in the form of the Holy Scriptures, and you hear it every Sunday from the pulpit. How would you ever have come to love Him if He had not sent His Gospel to you?

The gift of His Son Jesus, and the providence that brings the message of mercy to the saved, are evident causes of man's love for God. However, even more than this, Christ died and the Gospel is preached, and yet some men do not love Him. Why not? They do not love Him because of *"the hardness of their hearts"* (Mark 3:5).

But, are the hearts of those who do love Him naturally better than those who do not? I dare not say so. There is no believer who would ask me to trace his own love to any inherent human quality. Rather, I must trace it to the influence of the Holy Spirit. The revelation of the love of God in Christ Jesus affects the heart, creating faith and love and every grace in the soul.

If you love God, it is with no love of your own, but with the love that He has planted in your heart. Unrenewed human nature is a soil in which love for God will not grow naturally. There must be a taking away of the rock and a supernatural change of the barren ground into good soil. Then, as a rare plant from another land, love must be planted in your heart and sustained by divine power, or else it never will be found there. No love for God in this world is of the right kind except that which is created and formed in the soul by the love of God.

The Combined Doctrines of Grace

Put the two truths together—that the love of God is first, and that the love of God is the cause of our love—and I think you will understand what are commonly called the doctrines of grace. These doctrines are so consistent with the Christian's experience that the older a believer becomes and the more deeply he searches into divine truth, the more he praises the grace of God for his salvation. He is also more inclined to believe in those precious truths that magnify, not the free will of man, but the free grace of the Ever Blessed.

I want no better statement of my own doctrinal belief than *"We love him, because he first loved us."* I know it has been said that He loved us on the foresight of our faith and love and holiness. Of course, the Lord had a clear foresight of all these, but He also foresaw our lack of love, our lack of faith, our wanderings, and our sins. Surely His foresight in one direction must operate just as well as His foresight in the other direction.

God did not foresee any love for Him arising out of ourselves. He only foresaw that we would believe because He gave us faith; He foresaw that we would repent because His Spirit would work repentance in us; He foresaw that we would love because He created that love within us. Is there anything in His foresight that can account for His giving us such things?

The case is self-evident: His foresight of what He means to do cannot be His reason for doing it. His own eternal purpose has made the gracious difference between the saved and those who willfully perish in sin. Let us give all the glory to His holy name, for to Him all the glory belongs. His preventing grace must have all the honor.

Experimental Information

All True Believers Love God

Secondly, we will use the text for experimental information. First, we learn that all true believers love God. *"We love him,"* and we all love him for one reason, *"because he first loved us."* All the children of God love their Father. Of course, they do not all feel an equal love, or as much love as they should. Yet who among us does? We sometimes lead others to doubt our love. Indeed, it is well for us to examine ourselves even as Christ examined Peter, and said, *"Simon, son of Jonas, lovest thou me?"* (John 21:16).

However, there is love in the heart of every true-born child of God. It is as needful to spiritual life as blood is to natural life. No one born into the kingdom of God is born destitute of love for God. You may be deficient in some virtues (you should not be), yet the roots of them may be in you. But, if you are without love, you are *"as sounding brass, or a tinkling cymbal"* (1 Cor. 13:1). You may give your body to be burned and all your goods to feed the poor (1 Cor. 13:3); yet if you do not love God, the mark of God's sheep is not upon you, and your spot is not the spot of His children (Deut. 32:5). Rest assured that anyone who is born of God also loves God (1 John 4:7).

Our Love Is One of Gratitude

Observe carefully the *kind* of love that is essential to every Christian: *"We love him, because he first loved us."* Much has been said about disinterested, or unconditional, love for God. There may be such a thing, and it may be very admirable, but it is not mentioned here. I trust we know what it is to love God because of His superlative excellence and goodness. Surely, the more we know Him, the more we will love Him for who He is. Yet, unless we love Him because He first loved us, whatever other sort of love we may have or think we have does not prove us to be children of God.

Disinterested love, if it is genuine, will grow up in us afterwards. That, however, is

42

not essential, nor should we praise it excessively. Loving God because He first loved us is a sufficient evidence of grace in our souls. Gratitude has been denounced as a mean virtue, but it is actually a noble emotion and one of the most potent of spiritual motives. We can love God admiringly because of who He is, but a grateful love for God must run alongside that admiring love because He first loved us. Otherwise, we lack what John said is to be found in all the saints.

Do not worry yourself about loving Him to any supposed higher degree, but make sure you love Him because He first loved you. You might not be able to rise to the heights to which others have ascended, because you are as yet only a babe in grace. Yet, you are safe enough if your love is of this simple character: it loves because it is loved. Within this humble form of love dwells a gracious sense of unworthiness, so needful to a true Christian. We did not deserve the love that God continually sheds upon us, and we must have this humility, or we lack one mark of a child of God.

Also in this humble form of love is a clear recognition of the fact that the Lord's love is graciously bestowed. This, too, is essential to a Christian, for it becomes the main source of his obedience and affection. If a man only loves me as much as I deserve to be loved, I do not feel myself to be under any very strong obligation, and consequently I do not feel any very intense gratitude. In contrast, because the Lord's love is pure grace and comes to us who are utterly undeserving of it, we love Him in return. See whether such a humble, grateful love for God dwells in your heart, for it is a vital point.

Evidence of Our Salvation

Love for God, wherever it is found, is a sure evidence of the salvation of its possessor. If you love the Lord in the sense described, then He loved you first and loves you now. You need no other evidence except that you love Him to be sure that you abide in His love.

A short time ago, I was told a story of the famous preacher, Robert Hall. He charmed the most learned by the majesty of his eloquence, but he was as simple as he was great, and he was never happier than when conversing with other believers about experimental godliness. Having been preaching at Clipstone, he was on his way home on horseback when he was stopped at the little village of Sibbertoft by a heavy snowfall. The good man who kept the Black Swan, a little village hostelry, came to him and implored the preacher to take refuge beneath his roof, assuring him that it would give him great joy to welcome him.

Knowing him to be one of the most sincere Christians in the neighborhood, Mr. Hall therefore got off his horse and went into the little inn. The good man was delighted to provide for him a bed, a stool, and a candlestick in the prophet's chamber, for that rustic inn contained such an apartment.

After Mr. Hall had rested awhile by the fire, the landlord said, "You must stop here all night, sir; and if you do not mind I will call in a few of my neighbors. If you could give us a sermon in my taproom, they will all be glad to hear you."

"So let it be, sir," said Mr. Hall, and so it was. The barroom became his cathedral, and the "Black Swan" sign became the gospel banner. The peasants came together, and the man of God poured out his soul before them wondrously. They would never forget it, for to hear Mr. Hall was an event in any man's life. After all the peasants were gone, Mr. Hall sat down, and there came over him a fit of depression, which he strove to dismiss by conversation with his host.

"Ah, sir," said the great preacher, "I am much burdened and am led to question my own condition before God. Tell me now what you think is a sure evidence that a man is a child of God."

"Well, Mr. Hall," said the plain man, "I am sorry to see you so tried; you doubt yourself, but nobody else has any doubt about you. I hope the Lord will cheer and comfort you, but I am afraid I am not qualified to do it."

"Never mind, friend, never mind. Tell me, what do you think is the best evidence of a child of God?"

"Well, I should say, sir," said the innkeeper, "if a man loves God, he must be one of God's children."

"Say you so," said the mighty preacher, "then it is well with me," and he began to magnify the Lord. His hearer afterwards said that it was wonderful to hear him, for he went on with glowing earnestness for about an hour, declaring the loveliness of God.

"O sir," said he who told me the tale, "you should have heard him. He said, 'Love God, sir. Why, I cannot help loving Him; how could I do otherwise?' Then he went on to speak about the Almighty and His love and grace, extolling the Lord's greatness and goodness and glory in redemption and all that He did for His people, until he said, 'Thank you, thank you, my friend. If love for Him is an evidence of being God's child, I know I have it, for I cannot help loving Him. I take no credit to myself; He is such a lovely being and has done so much for us that I should be more brutish than any man if I did not love and adore Him.'"

What cheered that good man's heart may, perhaps, cheer yours. If you are loving God, you must have been loved by God first: true love could not have come into your heart in any other conceivable way. You may rest assured that you are the object of His eternal choice.

But, oh, if you do not love God, then think for a minute upon your state! Hear of God, but not love Him? You must be deaf. Know anything about His character, but not adore Him? Your heart must be like the heart of Nabal when it was turned into a stone (1 Sam. 25:37). See God in Christ bleeding on the cross for His enemies, and yet not love Him? You cannot be guilty of a worse offense than this! Will you not acknowledge the truest form of love?

It is said that a man cannot feel that he is loved without in some measure returning the flame, but what can I say of a mind that beholds Christ's love yet feels no love in return? It is brutish; it is devilish. God have mercy upon it! Such an unloving heart ought to breathe a prayer and say, "Lord, forgive me, and by Your Holy Spirit renew me, and give me the ability to say, 'I also in my humble fashion love God because He first loved me.'"

Practical Direction

Thirdly, we will use the text for practical direction. If you do not love God at present, I trust that you yet desire to do so. Well, dear friend, the text tells you *how* to love God.

Perhaps you say, "Oh, I will love God when I have improved my character and when I have attended to the external duties of religion." But, are you going to find love for God within yourself? Does such a love originate with you? "No," you say. How, then, will you get it? You may go often to an empty iron safe before you will bring a thousand dollar bill out of it. Likewise, you will look a long time into your own heart before you will bring out of it a love for God that is not there.

Meditate upon His Love

What is the way by which a heart may be made to love God? The text shows us the method of the Holy Spirit. He reveals the love of God to the heart, and then the heart loves God in return. If, then, you desire to love God, use the method that the text suggests. Meditate upon the great love God has for man, especially upon this:

> *For God so loved the world, that he gave his only begotten Son, that whosoever believeth in him should not perish, but have everlasting life.*   *(John 3:16)*

This is a vast love. The only thing required of you for salvation is that you be nothing and trust Christ to be everything. Even the faith that He gives you is a gift of His Spirit (Eph. 2:8), so that the plan of salvation is carried out entirely in love.

If you want to repent, do not consider your sin so much as the love of Jesus in suffering for your sin. If you desire to believe, do not study the doctrine so much as study the person of Jesus Christ upon the cross. If you desire to love, perpetually think over the great love of Jesus Christ in laying down His life for His worthless foes, until it breaks your heart. The love of God is the birthplace of holy love. It is not there in your heart, where you are attempting to create love in the carnal mind. Your attempts are fruitless, because the carnal mind cannot be reconciled to God (Rom. 8:7).

Love must be born in the heart of Jesus, and then it can come down to you. You cannot force your mind to believe even a common thing, nor can you sit there and say, "I will love so and so," of whom you know nothing. Faith and love are second steps arising out of former steps. *"Faith cometh by hearing"* (Rom. 10:17), and love comes by contemplation.

Love flows out of a sense of the love of Christ in the soul, even as wine flows from the clusters in the winepress. Go to the fragrant garden of redeeming love, and tarry there until your own garments are made to smell of myrrh and aloe and cassia. There is no way of sweetening yourself except by tasting the sweetness of Jesus Christ. The honey of His love will make your whole nature to be as a honeycomb; every cell of your being will drop sweetness.

If we wish to sustain the love we have received, we must, again, meditate upon His love. At the present moment, you are loving God and desire still to love Him. Be wise, then, and feed love with love, as it is its own best food. This is the honey that will keep your sweetness sweet; this is the fire that will keep your flame flaming. If we could be separated from the love of Christ, our love would die out like a streetlamp that has been cut off from the main power source. He who quickened us into the life of love must keep us alive, or we will become loveless and lifeless.

Perhaps, by chance, your love has grown somewhat cold. If you long to revive it, do not begin by doubting God's love for you. That is not the way of reviving, but of weakening love. Instead, believe in divine love, and take your focus off the coldness of your heart. Trust in Jesus Christ as a sinner if you cannot rejoice in Him as a saint, and you will get your love back again.

Imagine a flowing fountain, gushing with a constant stream. If I bring a pitcher and set it down, the stream rushes into it and fills it until it overflows. In this manner our souls ought to be filled with the love of Christ. However, you have taken away your pitcher, it has become empty, and now you say to yourself, "This pitcher is empty. There is nothing here! What shall I do?" Do? Why, do what you did at first. Go and set it under the flowing stream, and it will soon be full again; it will never get full by your removing it to a dry place.

Doubting is the death of love; only by the hand of faith can love be fed with the bread of heaven. Your tears will not fill the pitcher. You may groan into it, but sighs and moans will not fill it. Only the flowing fountain can fill the vacuum. Believe that God loves you still. Even if you are not a saint, believe in the mighty love of Christ toward sinners. Entrust yourself to Him, and then His love will come pouring in until your heart is full again to overflowing.

If you want to rise to the very highest state of love for Christ, if you desire to enjoy ecstatic delights or to be perfectly consecrated, if you aim at an apostle's self-denial or at a martyr's heroism, or if you would be as like to Christ as the spirits are in heaven—no tool can ingrain this image in you but love, and no force can fashion you into the model of Christ Jesus except the love of Christ shed abroad in your soul by the Holy Spirit (Rom. 5:5). Keep to this, then, as a matter of practical direction. Dwell in the love God has for you so that you may feel intense love for God in return.

Demonstrate Your Love for Him

Once more, as a practical direction, if you love God, show it as God showed His love to you. You cannot do so in the same degree, but you may in the same manner. God loved the worthless: you, too, should love the worthless. God loved His enemies: love your enemies (Matt. 5:44). The Lord loved them practically: love not in word only, but *"in deed and in truth"* (1 John 3:18). He loved them to the point of self-sacrifice, so that Jesus gave Himself for us: love to sacrifice of yourself, also.

Love God so much that you could die a thousand deaths for Him. Love Him to the point that you make no provision for the flesh (Rom. 13:14), but live alone for His glory. Let your heart burn with a flame that consumes you until the zeal of God's house has eaten you up (Ps. 69:9). *"We love him, because he first loved us."* Therefore, let us love Him as He loved us. Let His love be both motive and model to us.

> Lov'd of my God, for him again,
> With love intense I burn;
> Chosen of him ere time began,
> I choose him in return.

An Argumentative Defense

We Have License to Love Him So

Our text suggests to us, fourthly, an argumentative defense. You will see what I mean when I say, first, that our love for God seems to want an apology. We have heard of an emperor casting eyes of love upon a peasant girl. It would have been monstrous for her to have first looked up to him as likely to be her husband; everybody would have thought her senseless had she done so. However, when the monarch looked down upon her and asked her to be his queen, that was another thing. She could love him because he first loved her.

My soul often says, "O God, I cannot help loving You, but may I? May this poor heart of mine be allowed to send up its love to You? May I, polluted and defiled, nothingness and emptiness and sinfulness, say, 'Almighty as You are, yet do I love You, my God'? *'Holy, holy, holy,'* is the salutation of the seraphim (Rev. 4:8), but may I say, 'I love You, O my God'?" Yes, I may, because He first loved me. Love has a license to soar so high.

> Yet I may love you too, O Lord,
> Almighty as thou art,
> For you have stoop'd to ask of me
> The love of my poor heart.

Just as the spouse was asked,

> *What is thy beloved more than another beloved, O thou fairest among women? what is thy beloved more than another beloved, that thou dost charge us?* (Song 5:9)

so might anyone inquire of us, "What is this passion that you have for God, this love you bear to His incarnate Son?" In that case, we have a conclusive argument. We may reply,

"We love Him, because He first loved us. If you knew that He loved you, if you knew that He has done for you what He has done for us, you would love Him, too. You would not want to ask us why. Rather, you would wonder why you do not love Him as we do."

His love if all the nations knew,
Sure the whole world will love him too.

We will never have the need for any other defense for loving God than this: *because he first loved us.*"

Grace Brings Us to Holiness

In 1 John 4:19, we also have an argument for the lover of the old orthodox faith. It has been said by some that the doctrines of grace lead to licentiousness, but our text is an excellent shield against that attack. We believe that the Lord loved us, first and most freely, not because of our tears or prayers, nor because of our foreseen faith, nor because of anything in us. Rather, He loved us first. Well, what comes out of that? Do we therefore say, "If He loved us when we were in sin, let us *continue in sin that grace may abound*'" (Rom. 6:1), as some have wickedly said? God forbid! The inference we draw is, *"We love him, because he first loved us."*

Some can be swayed to morality by fear, but the Christian is sweetly drawn to holiness by love. We love Him, not because we are afraid of being cast into hell if we do not. That fear is gone, for we who are justified by God can never be condemned. (See Romans 8:33–34.) We love Him, not because we are afraid of missing heaven, for the inheritance is given to all who are joint-heirs with Jesus Christ. (See Romans 8:16–17.)

Does this blessed security lead us to carelessness? No, but the more we see the greatness and the infinity of the love of God, the more we love Him in return. That love is the basis of all holiness and the groundwork of a godly character. The doctrine of grace, though often maligned, has proved to be the grandest stimulus to heroic virtue in the hearts of believers, and whoever claims otherwise does not know what he says.

A Description of Christianity

Last of all, our Scripture reference is a noble argument to silence a gainsaying world. Do you see what a wonderful text we have here? It is a description of Christianity. Men say they are weary of the old faith, and they beg us to advance with the times. How should we reply? They want something better, do they? Are the philosophers who exploit the weaknesses of the age going to give it a better religion than Christianity? Let us see. We would, however, have to wait very long before their false promises come close to fulfillment.

Let us rather look at what we have already. Our text is a circle. Love descends from heaven down to man, and love ascends from man to God, and so the circle is completed. The text talks only of love. We love the Lord, and He loves us. This resembles Anacreon's harp, which resounded love alone. There is no word of strife, selfishness, anger, or envy; all is love, and love alone.

Now, it comes to pass that out of this love between God and His people there grows love for others, because *"he who loveth God love*[s] *his brother also"* (1 John 4:21). The ethical essence of Christianity is love, and the great master doctrine that we preach when we preach Jesus Christ is this: God has loved us, we love God, and now we must love one another.

What could be a greater Gospel than this? This kind of love will put aside your cannons and your swords. When men love God and love each other, is there any need for all the blood-stained pageantry of war? This love will put an end to bondage, for who will oppress and domineer when he has learned to love the image of God in every man?

Christianity is the Magna Carta of the universe. It holds the true "Liberty, Equality, and Fraternity," for which men will vainly seek in politics. Here is the Communism that will injure no man's rights, but will respect every man's griefs and succor every man's needs. Here is, indeed, the birth principle of the golden age of peace and joy, when the lion shall eat straw like the ox and the weaned child shall put his hand on the viper's den. (See Isaiah 11:7–8.)

Spread it, then, and let it circulate throughout the whole earth: God's love first, our love for Him next, and then the universal love that includes men of any color, any class, and any name. Love calls upon itself to love both God and man, because God first loved us.

The Lord bless this meditation to you, by His Spirit, for Christ's sake. Amen.

3

A Blessed Gospel Chain

Jesus answered and said unto him,
If a man love me, he will keep my words:
and my Father will love him,
and we will come unto him,
and make our abode with him.
—*John 14:23*

We have seen how our love for God is caused by His love for us, but knowing the origin of love is not enough. Something must be done with that love: we must also keep His words. This is the start of a chain that results in a closer relationship with our Lord and Savior, one in which we are not separated from Him in the least.

This a blessed chain of gospel experience. Our text is not meant for the men of the world who have their portion in this life. It is meant for the chosen, the called, the faithful, who are brought into the inner circle of Christ's disciples and taught to understand the mysteries of His kingdom. It was in answer to the question of Judas as to how Christ would manifest Himself to His own and not to the world (John 14:22) that the above words were spoken.

Christ explained that He would be manifested by certain marks and signs to those who were His own people. His people would be those who love Him and keep His commandments, and so win the approval of the Father. Then, the Father and the Son would come to these loving and obedient disciples and make their abode with them. God grant that all of us may be able to take each of the steps mentioned here, so that our Lord may manifest Himself to us as He does not unto the world!

The subject of this particular chapter is one that the preacher cannot handle without the people. He must have God's people with him in spirit to help him while he deals with such a topic as this. In some church services, there are certain places where the minister tells his congregation, "Repeat after me," so that he is somewhat of a choir director leading the rest of the congregation. In a similar style, I want you, as the Holy Spirit enables you, to bend all your thoughts and energies in this direction and to climb step-by-step with me to the distinct spiritual platforms in the chain. Ascend from one to the next by the Spirit's gracious aid, so that your fellowship may be with the Father, and with His Son, Jesus Christ.

"If a Man Love Me"

Our text begins with the first link in this golden chain, namely, love for Christ: *"If a man love me."* This "if" seems to stand at the entrance of our text, like a watchman at the gate of a palace, to prevent anybody from entering who ought not to enter. It is an "if" with which to examine yourself, for not everyone loves the Lord Jesus Christ. If you cannot answer in the affirmative the question asked by the lips of Jesus himself, *"Lovest thou me?"* (John 21:16), you have nothing to do with the rest of the verse.

Indeed, what have you to do with any of the privileges revealed in the Bible or with any of the blessings promised there if you are without love for Christ? Let that "if" stand, then, like the cherubim at the gates of the

61

garden of Eden (Gen. 3:24), to keep you from intruding where you have no right to go if you do not love the Lord Jesus Christ. Keep in mind, *"If a man love me."*

Are you a lover of the Lord? Do not set that question aside, but answer it honestly in His sight, for there are some who only pretend to love Him, but really do not. Some make loud professions, but their language is hypocritical, or their conduct is not consistent therewith. Do you love the Lord Jesus with your whole heart? He is well worthy of your love, so consider the question seriously, *"Lovest thou me?"*

There are some, too, who are Christ's disciples only by lip service. All they give Him is a cold-hearted assent to His teaching. Their heads are convinced, and, in a measure, their lives are not altogether inconsistent with their profession, but their hearts are dead. Or, if they are at all alive, they are like the church of Laodicea, neither cold nor hot, but lukewarm—a state that Christ abhors (Rev. 3:16). Christ must occupy the throne of our hearts and be the best loved of all, or else we lack that which is essential to true Christianity.

"If a man love me," says Christ. So, do you love Him? I do not ask whether you love His offices, though I hope you do. You love the Prophet, the Priest, the King, the Shepherd,

the Savior, and whatever other title He assumes. Each of these names is music to your ears—but do you love Christ Himself? I will not ask whether you love His work, especially the great redemption that entails innumerable blessings. I hope you do, but it is a personal love for Christ that is spoken of here.

Jesus says, *"If a man love me."* Have you personally realized Christ as still alive and gone into heaven, and soon to come again in all the glory of His Father and of the holy angels? Say, brother or sister, do you love Him? *"If,"* says Christ, *"If a man love me."* So it is right and wise for each one of us to put that question to ourselves, even though we know that we can answer it satisfactorily and say,

Yes, I love you, and adore;
Oh, for grace to love you more!

If there is any doubt about the matter, we ought to ask the question again and again and again and not let ourselves escape until there is a definite answer given one way or another. Ask of your own heart, "Do I really love the Savior?" Ask yourself this question; and if you answer that you do love Him, let your love well up like a mighty geyser, a hot spring that leaps up to a great height. So let the hot spring of your love for Jesus leap up now, and say to Him,

> My Jesus, I love thee,
>   I know thou art mine,
> For thee all the follies
>   of sin I resign;
> My gracious Redeemer,
>   my Savior art thou,
> If ever I loved thee,
>   my Jesus, 'tis now.

If you can do so, then you may add,

> I will love thee in life,
>   I will love thee in death,
> And praise thee as long
>   as thou lendest me breath;
> And say when the death-dew
>   lies cold on my brow,
> If ever I loved thee,
>   my Jesus, 'tis now.

Remember from the previous chapter that, if you do love Him, He must have loved you first. Think of His ancient love, the love that was fixed upon you before the earth began. He saw you in the glass of futurity, He beheld all that you would be in the ruinous fall of Adam, and He foreknew all of your personal transgressions. Yet He loved you, notwithstanding all. Think of Him, when the fullness of time had come, stripping Himself of all His glory and descending from the throne of infinite majesty to the manger of humiliation.

Think of Him as a babe, swaddled in His weakness. Will you not love Him who became God incarnate for you? Think of Him all through His life: a life of poverty, for He had nowhere to lay His head (Matt. 8:20); a life of rejection, for *"he came unto his own, and his own received him not"* (John 1:11); a life of pain, for He bore our sicknesses (Matt. 8:17); a life of dishonor, for He was despised and rejected by men (Isa. 53:3).

Think of Him in the garden of Gethsemane. (See Mark 14:32–39.) Will your love not be stirred as you watch the bloody sweat and hear His groans and mark His tears, as He pleads with God until He prevails? Follow Him to the judgment seat, and hear Him there charged with blasphemy (Matt. 26:65), if you can bear it. Then see the soldiers, as they spit in His face and mock Him, while they thrust a reed into His hand for a scepter, and put on His brow a crown of thorns as His only diadem (Matt. 27:29). See Him tied up to be scourged (Mark 15:15), until the cruel thongs lacerate and tear His precious flesh and He suffers indescribable agonies.

When you have followed Him so far, go further still, stand at the foot of the cross, and mark the crimson stream that flows from His hands and feet and side. Stand and watch Him when the soldier's spear has pierced His heart and made the blood and water flow forth (John 19:34) for your pardon and cleansing. Did He suffer all this for you, and you do not love Him in return? Can I not tell that "if" to get out of the way and let you pass in, so that you may take the next step?

Track Him as He rises from the grave for you, as He ascends to heaven for you and obtains great gifts for you. Listen as He pleads for you before His Father's face. Follow Him to the throne from which, as King of Kings and Lord of Lords, He governs all things for you. In heaven He prepares many mansions for His people (John 14:2). He readies Himself to come to earth a second time so that He may receive His people unto Himself, that where He is they may be also for evermore (John 14:3).

As you think of all this, love the Lord, you who are His saints. You who have been washed in His blood, love Him! You who are wearing the spotless robe of His righteousness, love Him. You who call him "Husband," love Him, you who are married to Him, united in bonds that can never be severed. If this is true of you, let us pass on to the next point, that of keeping Christ's words.

"He Will Keep My Words"

Treasuring His Words

"If any man love me," says Christ, *"he will keep my words."* Let us see how far we have kept His words. I trust that, first, we keep His words by *treasuring* them and *prizing them.* I hope that we venerate every word that Christ has ever uttered. I trust that we desire to treasure up every syllable that He has ever spoken. There is not a word of His, recorded in the Gospels or in any other part of the Bible, that is not more valuable than much fine gold (Ps. 119:72).

Trying to Know His Words

I trust that we keep Christ's words, next, by trying to know them. Are you a diligent student of the Word? Do you search the Scriptures? Do you live upon the truth that the Lord has spoken? You should do so, for every word that comes out of His mouth is the true food of your soul. (See Matthew 4:4.) I must ask you whether you are doing these two things: are you keeping Christ's words by prizing them, and are you seeking to be so familiar with them that you know what His words are?

Finding the Meaning of His Words

Then, next, do you endeavor to lift the latch, to find your way into the inner meaning of His words? Do you crack the shell to get at the core? Does the Spirit of God lead you into all truth (John 16:13), or are you content with the rudiments of the faith? The way to keep Christ's words is by endeavoring, to your very utmost, to understand the meaning of those words.

Keeping His Words in Your Heart

Then, when you know the meaning of them, do you seek to keep them in your heart? Do you love what Christ has spoken, so that you delight to know what it is and love it because it is His doctrine? Will you sit at His feet and receive the instruction that He is willing to impart? Have you reached that stage where you love even His rebukes? If His words come home to you and sharply reprove you, do you love them even then and lay bare your heart before Him, that you may feel more and more the faithful wounds of your beloved Savior?

Do you also love His precepts? Are they as sweet to you as His promises? Or, if you could do as you wish, would you cut them out of the Bible and get rid of them? It is proof that grace has been generously given to us when even the smallest word uttered by Christ is more precious to us than all the diamonds in the world, and we feel that we only want to know what He has said and to love whatever He has spoken.

Keeping His Words through Your Actions

"If a man love me, he will keep my words." This declaration of our Lord suggests the question: "Do we keep His words practically?" That is an important point, for you will not be able to get any further if you stumble here. Do you endeavor, in a practical way, to keep all His moral precepts? Are you trying to be like Him as far as you can in your life, or are you selfish, unkind, worldly? Are you endeavoring to follow His example by following His steps? Come, answer honestly. Is this the object of your being?

Are you seeking to be molded by the Holy Spirit in that way? Are you practically keeping Christ's words as to the precepts of the

Gospel? Have you believed on Him? Believing on Him, have you been baptized according to His command? Being baptized, do you come to His table, according to His bidding: *"This do in remembrance of me"* (Luke 22:19)? Or do you turn on your heel and say that these are non-essential things?

Beloved, if your heart is right with God, you will want to know all His words and put them into practice. The words of any earthly church are only the words of men. Search and find the words of Christ; and wherever they lead you, even though you are the only one who has ever been led in that way, follow wherever He leads.

You cannot take the next step unless you can deliberately say, "Yes, Lord, Your words were found, and I drank in their full meaning. Your Word was unto me the joy and rejoicing of my heart; for I am called by Your name, O Lord God of Hosts. I long to walk blamelessly in all Your statutes and ordinances, even to the end of my days." (See Jeremiah 15:16 and Ezekiel 11:20.)

You may err; you may make mistakes; you may commit sin. But, the intent of your heart must be that, having loved the Lord, you will keep His words in those various senses that I have mentioned.

If you have been enabled to pass through these two gates, you may now come to the next one, which tells us of a high privilege and a great joy: *"He will keep my words, and my Father will love him."*

"And My Father Will Love Him"

Harmony in Loving the Son

What wonderful words these are: *"My Father will love him"*! It is quite certain that He will do so, for when a man loves Jesus, he is in harmony with the eternal Father Himself. The Father's love is fixed upon His only begotten Son. He has loved the Son from eternity, for they are one in their essential deity. However, since Jesus has been obedient unto death, *"even the death of the cross"* (Phil. 2:8), we cannot imagine the Father's satisfaction in our risen and ascended Lord.

This is a deep subject, and there is no human mind that can ever fathom the depths of it and tell how truly and how wonderfully the Father loves His everlasting Son. So, you see that if we love Jesus Christ, our hearts meet the heart of God, for the Father also loves Him. When you have been trying to praise Jesus, have you ever felt that you are doing, in your feeble way, just what God has always been doing in His infinite way? The ever-blessed Spirit is continually glorifying Jesus. When you are doing the same, God and you, though with very unequal footsteps, are treading the same path and are in harmony with one another.

Harmony in Character

Then, besides the fact that you have an affinity with the Father in having one object of love, you are also in accord with Him as to character. Jesus said, *"If a man love me, he will keep my words."* Well, when you are keeping Christ's words—when the divine Spirit is making you obedient to Jesus and like Jesus—you are treading the path where your heavenly Father would have you walk, and therefore He loves you.

Let me make a clear distinction here. I am not now writing about the general love of God toward all mankind—the love of benevolence and beneficence that is displayed even toward the thankless and the evil. Neither am I addressing just now the essential love of God toward His own elect whom He loves, regardless of their character, because of His own sovereign choice of them from eternity. Rather, I am considering the special love that God, as a Father, has toward His own children.

A father will often say to his child, "If you do this or that, I will love you." Yet, you know that a father will love his child as his child, and he must always do so even if the child's character is not all that the father desires it to be. However, what an amazing love a father has for a good, dutiful, obedient child! It is a love of which he talks to him again and again, a love that he manifests to him in many sweet and kindly words. It is a love that the father displays in many ways that he would not otherwise have done. He bestows upon the child many favors that would not have been safe to bestow had the child been naughty and disobedient.

Likewise, our heavenly Father exercises wise discipline in His house. He has rods for His children who disobey Him, and He has smiles for His children who keep His commands. If we walk contrary to Him, He has told us that He will walk contrary to us; but if our ways please Him, there are many choice favors that He bestows upon us. This teaching is not suggestive of legal bondage, for we *are not under law, but under grace*" (Rom. 6:14). This is the law of God's house under the rule of grace.

For instance, if a man keeps the Lord's commandments, he will have power with God in prayer. But, when a man lives habitually in sin, or even occasionally falls into sin, he cannot pray so as to prevail, and he cannot win the ear of God as he used to do. If you have offended the Lord in any way, you know that you cannot enjoy the Gospel as you did before you so sinned. The Bible, instead of smiling upon you, seems to threaten you in every line; it seems to rise up, as if written in letters of fire, and burn its way into your conscience.

It is certainly true that the Lord deals differently with His own children according to their behavior and character. So, when a man keeps Christ's words, his character is such that God can take an approving delight in him and, in this sense, can love him. It is in a case such as this that the Father will let us know that He loves us, that He will assure us of that love, and that He will shed it abroad in our hearts by the Holy Spirit (Rom. 5:5).

He will give us special blessings, perhaps in providence, but certainly in grace. He will create for us special joy and rejoicing (Is. 65:18), He will exalt our horn (Ps. 89:17), and He will set our feet upon the high places of the earth (2 Sam. 22:34). All things—even his trials—will be blessed to the man who walks aright with God; and the way to do that is to love Christ and to keep His words. Of such a man, Jesus says, *"My Father will love him."*

"We Will Come unto Him"

If you have passed through these three gates, you come to another, which bears the inscription, *"We will come unto him."* This is a singular use of the plural pronoun, "We." It is a proof of the distinct personalities of the Father and the Son. Jesus said, *"If a man love me"* (do not forget the previous links in this blessed gospel chain), *"he will keep my words: and my Father will love him."* Then follows this gracious assurance: *"We will come unto him."*

No Longer Separated

The first meaning of this is *distance removed*. There is no longer a gap between such a man and his God. He feels heavy in heart, perhaps, and thinks, "I cannot get near to God." But, he hears this comforting message: *"We will come unto him."* Soon, over all the mountains of division that there may have been in the past, the well-beloved comes like a doe over the hills. When God sees, in the distance, His child returning to Him, the great Father runs to meet him and embraces him and holds him close to His heart.

How wonderful a meeting this is! Christ and His Father, by the Holy Spirit, come to pay the believer a most gracious visit. Yes, if you are living in love for Christ and are keeping His words, there will not be any distance separating you from the Father and the Son. The text, *"We will come unto him,"* will be blessedly fulfilled in your life.

Honored by the Father and the Son

And, while it means distance removed, it also means *honor conferred*. Many a great nobleman has beggared himself so that he might receive a prince or a king into his house. The entertainment of royalty has meant the mortgaging of his estates. That is a poor return for the honor of receiving a visit from his sovereign.

But, see how different it is with us. The obedient lover of the Lord Jesus Christ has the Father and the Son to visit him, and he is greatly enriched by their coming. He may be very poor, but Jesus says, *"We will come unto him."* He may be obscure and illiterate, but Jesus says, *"We will come unto him."*

Do you know what this coming means? Did you ever know the Son to come to you with His precious blood applied to your conscience, until you realized that every one of your sins was forgiven? Have you taken Jesus up in your arms, spiritually, as old Simeon did literally, and said with him, *"Lord, now lettest thou thy servant depart in peace according to thy word, for mine eyes have seen thy salvation"* (Luke 2:29–30)? Has Jesus seemed to be as near to you as one who sat on the same chair with you and talked with you in familiar conversation? It has been so with some of us, and it has often been so.

His Love Realized Further

This also means *knowledge increased*. Jesus has revealed Himself to us by coming to us, even as He came to the two disciples on the way to Emmaus (Luke 24:15). When the Father comes to you in His divine relationship, does He not make you feel as one of His children? Does this cause you to realize that He loves you as truly as parents love their own children, only much more deeply and fervently than human love can ever be?

Have His hands not given you good things, as only He could give, so that you felt the divine Fatherhood very near to you? Has not the

Spirit of God, operating within you, made you cry, *"Abba, Father"* (Gal. 4:6), with an unstammering tongue?

"We will come unto him." The Savior will come, and the Father will come, and the blessed Spirit will represent them both in the believer's heart.

We Have His Assistance

So, *"We will come unto him"* means distance removed, honor conferred, and knowledge increased. It also means *assistance brought*; for, if the Father and the Son come to us, what more can we need? With their gracious presence in our souls, we have infinity and omnipotence on our side, and grace to help us in every time of need (Heb. 4:16).

"And Make Our Abode with Him"

Finally, the last clause of our text, and the sweetest of all, is: *"And make our abode with him."* Can you catch the full meaning of that phrase? Jesus says that the Father and the Son will come to us, as the three blessed ones came to Abraham at the tent door. Abraham entertained the Lord and His attendant angels (see Genesis 18:1–16), but they did not make their abode with him. They went on their way, and

Abraham was left in the plains of Mamre. God often visited Abraham and spoke familiarly with him, but our Savior's promise goes beyond that. He says, *"We will come unto him, and make our abode with him."*

He Will Dwell Together with Us

To make your abode with a person is for the both of you to live together in the same house and home. In this case, it means that the Lord will dwell continually within His people, His temple. *"We will come unto him, and make our abode with him."* I have turned that thought over and over again in my mind until I have got the sweetness of it into my heart. However, I cannot communicate it directly to your minds and hearts; only the Holy Spirit can do that.

See what this expression means. What knowledge of one another is implied here! Do you want to know a person? You must live with him. You do not really know anybody, however much you may think you know, until you have done so. But, oh, if the Father and the Son come and live with us, we will know them—we will know the Father and the Son!

This is not a privilege for carnal minds, nor is it for professing Christians who have not fulfilled the conditions laid down by our Lord.

But, it is for those who love Christ and keep His words, those who consciously live in the enjoyment of the Father's blessing and who have fellowship with the Father and with the Son by the Spirit. To these privileged individuals, God reveals Himself in His triune personality, and to them He will make known all that is in His covenant of love and mercy.

A Sacred Friendship with Us

This expression also implies a sacred friendship. When God comes to dwell with men, He does not dwell with His enemies. No, He dwells only with those who love Him, and where there is mutual affinity between them and Himself. If God the Father and God the Son indeed come to dwell with us, it will be a proof of wondrous love, dear familiarity, and intense friendship!

If you go to live with an earthly friend, it is quite possible for you to stay too long and to outstay your welcome. However, God knows all about the person with whom He comes to live. Jesus says, *"We will...make our abode with him,"* because He knows that His Spirit has purified and sanctified that heart and made it ready to receive Himself and His Father, too.

You remember how Jeremiah pleaded with the Lord not merely to be as a sojourner:

> *O the hope of Israel, the Savior thereof in
> time of trouble, why shouldest thou be as a
> stranger in the land, and as a wayfaring
> man that turneth aside to tarry for a
> night?* *(Jer. 14:8)*

Yet, this is not the way that the Father and the
Son deal with us, for Jesus says that they will
make their abode with us. Does this not imply
a very sacred friendship, indeed, between God
and His children?

He Will Accept Our Hospitality

It also reveals the complete acceptance of
the person before God. When anyone comes to
stay with you, it is taken for granted that you
exercise hospitality toward him. He eats and
drinks in your house; for the time, he makes
himself at home with you.

"But," you ask, "is it possible that God
would accept the hospitality of man?" Yes, it is.
Note the words of Christ Himself:

> *Behold, I stand at the door, and knock: if
> any man hear my voice, and open the door,
> I will come in to him, and will sup with
> him, and he with me.* *(Rev. 3:20)*

Oh, the blessedness of thus entertaining the
King of Kings! Then will He drink of my milk
and my wine, and eat the pleasant fruits that

are grown in the garden of my soul. (See Song of Solomon 4:16–5:1.)

Will that which I present to Him be acceptable to Him? It must be, or else He would not live in my house. When the Father and the Son come to dwell in the soul of the believer, then all that he does will be accepted. If he is himself accepted, it follows that his thoughts and his words, his prayers and his praises, his almsgiving and his labors for Christ will be accepted by both the Father and the Son.

What a blessed state for anyone to reach! For then it shall come to pass that this reception of God by us will be followed by a sevenfold reception of us by Him. When God the Father and God the Son make their abode in a man, the man cannot possibly continue to be just as he was when they first came to him. No, the Lord pays well for His lodging. Where He stays, He turns everything that He touches into gold. When He comes into a human heart, it may be dark, but He floods it with the light of heaven. It may have been cold before, but He warms it with the glory of His almighty love.

A man without the indwelling of God is like the bush in Horeb when it was only a bush. When the Father and the Son come to him, then it is with him as when the bush burned with fire, yet was not consumed (Exod. 3:2). The Lord brings heaven to you when He comes to you, and you are rich beyond simple bliss. All things are yours, for you are Christ's, and Christ is God's, and Christ and God have come to make their abode with you.

We Can Keep Him Near

Now, according to our Lord's promise, *"We will come unto him, and make our abode with him,"* it is implied that keeping Him near is the goal toward which this blessed gospel chain is directed. Perhaps you are wondering, "Is that all? Does the Lord wish to stop there?" Let me take your thoughts back for a minute to the earlier links in this blessed gospel chain. Let me remind you that it is only *"if a man love me,"* and it is only *"if he keep my words,"* that the Savior's promise applies: *"We will come unto him, and make our abode with him."* Then remember that you can do nothing except if you abide in the Lord and He in you (John 15:4).

Have the Father and the Son come to your heart? Then, I charge you, do nothing that might cause them to depart from you even for a moment. If you ever reach a conscious enjoyment of the divine indwelling, be jealous of your heart lest it should ever depart from your

Lord or drive Him from you. Say, with the spouse, *"I charge you, O daughters of Jerusalem, that ye stir not up, nor awake my love, until he please"* (Song 8:4).

"But," perhaps you ask, "can we keep Him? Can we keep Him forever?" I believe you can. By the blessed help of the Holy Spirit, who has taught you to love Him and to keep His words, you may have near and dear fellowship with your Lord month after month and year after year. I am sure that we have too low a standard of the possibilities of Christian fellowship, Christian enjoyment, and Christian living.

Aim at the highest conceivable degree of holiness; though you will not be perfect, never excuse yourselves because you are not. Always aim at something higher and yet higher still than you have already reached. Ask the Lord to come and abide with you forever. You will be happy Christians if you attain to this privilege and stay in that condition. We will be a blessed church if most or all of us should attain to it. I myself mean to aim for it. Will you, also?

Can you be content to live a life lower than is possible for you? I hope not. Rather, I hope that you will reach all of these steps that I have pointed out to you, and ask God in prayer to help you attain them.

Lord, help me to love Jesus. Set my soul on fire with love for Him. Lord, enable me to keep all His words and never to trifle with His truth in anything. And then, Father, look upon me with favor. Make me such that You can take delight in me. See the resemblance to Your Son in me, because You have made me to be like Him. Then, Father and Savior, come and abide with me forever and ever. Amen.

Such a prayer as that, truly presented, will be answered, and the Lord will take glory in it.

Go the Way of Salvation

But, some of you have nothing to do with this text because you do not love Christ. In that case, the first thing you have to do is not to think about loving Him, but about trusting Him. You know that the only way of salvation lies in trusting Christ. So, if you do not trust Him, you are not going the way of salvation.

Have you ever thought of what is involved in being an unbeliever? The apostle John said, *"He that believeth not God hath made him a liar; because he believeth not the record that God gave of his Son"* (1 John 5:10). Do you really want to make God out to be a liar? Surely, you do not. The thought of it is too horrible to be entertained even for a moment.

Well, then, believe His record concerning His Son. That record declares that He is the atonement for our sins. If you rely upon that and trust Him, then you are saved.

I often have the remark made to me, by an anxious soul, "But, sir, I cannot believe; I wish I could."

This is the answer that I generally give to the person who says something along those lines: "What! you cannot believe? You cannot believe God? Could you believe me?"

Of course, he responds, "Oh, yes, sir, I can believe you!"

I reply, "Yes, I suppose that is because you have confidence in my character and believe that I would not tell you a lie. Then, in the name of everything that is good and reasonable, how is it that you dare say that you cannot believe God? Is He a liar? Has He ever given you any cause to say to Him, 'I cannot believe You'? What do you mean? Give me some reason why you cannot believe God. What has He done that you cannot believe Him?"

Well, he does not quite see it in that light. But, still, he returns to saying, "I cannot believe."

Sinner, if Jesus Christ were present and He were to say to you, "Trust Me, and I will save you. Believe My promise, and you shall enter into eternal life," would you look Him in the face and say, "I cannot believe You"? If He asked you the question, "Why can you not believe Me?" what would be your reply? Surely, a man can believe what is true.

There have been times in my own life, since I have known the Savior, when it seemed that I could not doubt my Lord—as if I could not find a reason, even if I ransacked heaven and earth and hell, why I should doubt Him. I do not know any reason why I should not trust Christ. I cannot think of one. So, why do men continue this monstrous, unjust, ungenerous conduct?

"But," you say, "if I do trust my soul to Christ, will He save me?" Try Him, and see. You have His own promise that He will cast out none who come unto Him (John 6:37). So, if you believe in the Lord Jesus Christ this very moment, then at this very moment you are saved. What more needs to be said?

May the Holy Spirit cause you to cease your unbelief, which is making God a liar. May you now come and trust in Jesus, the Substitute and Surety for His people. Rest your weary heart in His loving arms, and it will be well with you forever and ever. May God bless you, for the sake of Christ Jesus! Amen.

4

God's Love for the Saints

Hereby perceive we the love of God,
because he laid down his life for us:
and we ought to lay down our
lives for the brethren.
—1 John 3:16

In the second chapter, we looked into 1 John 4:19 and discovered the meaning of *"We love him, because he first loved us."* Then, we learned how our love for Him begins a wonderful chain of events, where our love is reciprocated by both the Father and the Son, and where we share a very special relationship with them. Now, let us see what more we can learn about the love that God has for His people, the truest form of love.

True love cannot be passive for long. It is like fire, having an active nature. It must be at work. Love longs for expression, for it cannot be mute. Command it not to express itself, and you command it not to live. True love is not satisfied with expressing itself only in words. Of course, it uses words, but it is painfully conscious of their feebleness. The full meaning of love cannot be conveyed in any humble language. It breaks the backs of words and crushes them to atoms with all that it means.

Love must express itself in deeds, as the old proverb says, "Actions speak louder than words." Love also delights in making sacrifices. She rejoices in denying herself. In fact, the more costly the sacrifice, the more pleasure love takes in making it. She will not offer that which costs her nothing. She loves to endure pains and losses, for this is how she expresses herself best.

This is a general principle that applies to men and even to God Himself. *"God is love"* (1 John 4:8), and being love, He must display love. Merely speaking of His love is not enough. His love must manifest itself in action. More than that, God could not rest until He had made the greatest sacrifice that He could make and had given up His only begotten Son (John 3:16) to die in the place of sinners.

God does not come to us and say, "Men and women, I love you. You must believe that I love you, although I do nothing for you to prove My love." He does ask us to believe in His love, but He has given us abundant proofs of it. Therefore, He has a right to claim our belief in it. In a more literal translation of our text, the apostle of love tells us, "Hereby we come to know—we do know—'*the love of God, because he laid down his life for us.*'"

Just as we learn the love of others by seeing what they are prepared to sacrifice for us, so it is even with God Himself. We discover, discern, perceive, and are made to know the love that He bears to us by the fact that *"he laid down his life for us."* There are several ways in which we see God demonstrating this remarkable love to the saints, the first being His acts of love.

Acts of Love

First, I want to show you that there are many acts of God in which His love is very clear, but in which most men fail to see it. There are many of His acts, of which it might be said, "The love of God is clearly manifested in this." Yet, many men fail to perceive the love that lies behind the actions.

Our Christian Parentage

There are some of us who should have perceived God's love in the surroundings at our very birth. By this I mean that many of us owe much to Christian parentage. Many of us could truly say, in the words of the children's verse,

> I was not born, as thousands are,
> Where God was never known,
> And taught to pray a useless prayer
> To blocks of wood and stone.

What if your lot in life had been to be raised on the streets in poverty and violence instead of in a loving Christian home? What if you had been born a slave or a heathen? Perhaps you were fortunate enough to be raised by Christian parents, yet still you had to spend your childhood in the slums. Some of you think that your behavior has been virtuous and moral, but would you have been better than the boys that fill our reformatories if you had been raised in a ghetto without godly guidance? Would you have been better than those who crowd our prisons if you had had the same training, or lack of training, that they have had?

If you had been shown the example that was shown to them, if the taste of strong drink had been familiar to you almost from your birth, if the first thing you ever heard was blasphemy, if you had lived in the thieves' kitchen, do you think that you would have been any more clear of guilt than they have been?

When we look down on others, we ought to consider all their temptations and the conditions of their upbringing. We might almost admire them for not being worse than they are. It is a great struggle for some people to be honest. There are many people of whom we might think unfavorably. Nevertheless, they have suffered almost as martyrs do, and they have fought stern battles with temptation. If they have fallen somewhat, they are to be honored because they have not fallen still further.

What a blessing it was for some of us that, when we woke up in this world, we looked up into a face that smiled upon us and to lips that would eventually speak to us of Jesus Christ. The first example that we had was one that we wish to follow to this day. Our companions since our childhood have been of a godly order. And there are some in heaven now, who had much to do with the formation of our character and for whom we should always thank God.

Now, had we been wise, we would have understood the meaning of this arrangement.

We would have perceived the love of God for us in the very conditions in which we were born and brought up. Yet many of us did not see it. I would venture to say that some of you thought you were badly treated because you were placed in such a strict family. You were kept from what you regarded as the pleasures of life. Many a young man has felt tied to his mother's apron strings, while he saw other young men enjoying themselves. In addition, his father, like a grim jailer, was always watching closely, ready to reprimand him.

As a general rule, young men and women who have the high privilege of Christian parentage and training do not see the love of God in it. They often kick against it and wish they did not have to endure what they regard as a great hardship. That is the way we used to think of it in the days of our ignorance. But, now that God has opened our eyes, we can see the love of God in it all. We see how He has orchestrated things for our benefit.

The Ten Commandments

God has also revealed His love to us by giving us a wise and judicious law. The law of the Ten Commandments is a gift of great kindness, for it tells us the wisest and the happiest way of living. It forbids us only what would hurt us, and it withholds from us nothing that would be a real pleasure to us. The commands that say, *"Thou shalt,"* or *"Thou shalt not,"* are like the signs at some swimming pools that say, "Dangerous! Keep so many feet away from this spot."

God does not make laws denying us anything that would really be for our good. Imagine that a poisonous berry grows in your garden, and your child has been told not to eat it. If he is a wise child, he will understand that your instructions not to eat the berry were given out of love. If you had no care about him at all, you would allow him to eat whatever poison he chose. But, because you love him, you say to him, "My child, do not do this, because it will be to your serious injury. You could die if you disobey."

We ought to see the love of God in the gift of the law, but no one ever does until he is led to see the love of God in other ways. We rarely say of it, though we ought to do so, *"Hereby perceive we the love of God."*

Our Daily Health and Provisions

We have also had, in day-to-day provisions, countless manifestations of the love of God. If our eyes were really opened, every loaf of bread would come to us as a token of our Father's care, and every drop we drink would come as the gift of our Father's bounty. Are we not clothed by His love? Do we not breathe the air given to us by our Creator? Who else preserves us in health but our great Benefactor? Does it not prove His love that you are not lying sick in bed, or that you are not in the lunatic asylum, or that you are not standing on the edge of the grave, and that you are not in hell?

We are a mass of mercies and a mass of sins. We seem to be made of mercy and ingratitude mixed together. But, if the Lord will open our eyes, we will then see how boundless are the mercies we receive. We will begin to perceive His love. However, this is not the first place where man sees God's love. The cross is the lancet window through which the love of God is best seen. Until that window is opened, all the bounties of God's providence fail to convince us of His love.

Most men reap their harvests and yet never bless the God who gives the harvest. They drive the loaded wagons to the granaries, thresh out the wheat, and send it to be sold in the markets; but did you ever hear of a song of praise being sung in the marketplace when they brought the first new wheat to be sold?

Why, they would think we were all mad if, when the new wheat arrived, we all began to sing,

> Praise God from whom
> all blessings flow.

Most of them are probably cursing because the wheat has gone down a penny or two, and the poor people will possibly get their bread a little cheaper.

Praising God seems to have gone out of fashion. Philosophers tell us that the wheat springs up naturally and that God has nothing to do with it. They say that, regardless of rain or sun, the processes of nature are ruled by iron law with which God has no concern at all. According to their understanding, He has gone on vacation and left the world to manage itself. Or, He has wound it up like a watch, put it under His pillow, and gone to sleep. That is the philosopher's religion. As far as I am concerned, the philosophers may keep it, for it is not mine.

My religion believes in the God of the showers and the God of the sunshine and the God of the harvest. I believe in *the living God, who giveth us richly all things to enjoy* (1 Tim. 6:17). If our hearts were right with Him, we would *hereby perceive...the love of God,* but we do not. That perception comes to us only through a stained glass window—the window that was stained crimson by the precious blood of Christ. There, and only there, do we perceive the love of God, *"because he laid down his life for us."*

Laying Down His Life

That brings me to my second point, which is this: in the laying down of His life, Christ's love is best seen. I have already said that God's love ought to be seen in His many acts. But, according to the text, we *"hereby"* perceive *"the love of God, because he laid down his life for us."* It is universally admitted that there can be no greater proof of love than for a person to lay down his life for the object of that love (John 15:13). All sorts of sacrifices may be taken as proofs of affection, but the relinquishment of life is the supreme proof of love.

A man says that he loves his country. But, imagine that same man in the position of Curtius in the old Roman fable. The story tells that when a great chasm opened in the forum, it was declared that it could only be closed by the most precious thing in Rome being thrown into it. Curtius, fully armed and riding his charger, leaped into the chasm, which instantly closed. No one could doubt the love of such a man for his country.

If the question happened to be the love of humanity, we have the true story of a surgeon at Marseilles. The plague was raging through the city, and the people were dying by thousands. A bishop remained among them, discharging the last offices to the dying and cheering the living. Many of the surgeons of the town, who might have departed, lingered to wait upon the sick. At a consultation among them, it was resolved to make a *post mortem* examination of one of the worst cases of the pestilence. The question was, who should make it, for whoever did so would certainly die of the disease within a few hours.

One of them, to his honor, said, "My life is of no more value than that of any other man. Why should I not sacrifice it if, by doing so, I can discover the cause of this terrible malady and save this city?" He finished his grim task, wrote his notes about the case, then went to his home, and died. Nobody doubted that he loved the people of Marseilles, for he had laid down his life for them. If we acted as he did, nobody could doubt our love for our fellow creatures.

There is also the story of a mother's love that no one could doubt. In the time of disastrous floods, a mother climbed a hill, carrying her two small children. She reached a tree where she could rest, but then found that the tree was not strong enough to sustain herself and her two babes. So, placing them as far as she could out of harm's way, she leaped into the waters and soon sank. Nobody could doubt that mother's love when she laid down her life for her children.

Laying down one's life is the crowning proof of love. Even a devil's advocate will not rise up to dispute this truth. Those who can die for others must surely love those for whom they lay down their lives.

Now, our Lord Jesus Christ has proved His love for sinners by dying for them. Do you need me to tell you the story again? This is a story that should be read over and over again, anyway. It is written four times in the Gospels, but not once too often. The Son of God, for our sakes, died a felon's death and was mercilessly nailed to the cross to bleed away His life. Read that story again, and see how He proved His love to us.

He Surrendered Immortality

There are certain points about Christ's death that are very extraordinary and that are better proofs of love than those I have already mentioned. The first is this: Jesus did not ever have to die. When the Marseilles surgeon died, he only did then what he would have to do a few years afterwards. When the mother perished to save her children, she died only a few weeks, months, or years before her appointed time. Being mortal, we all must die. If we give our lives for others, we do not really give our lives. We simply pay the debt of nature a little while before it is due.

However, it was altogether different in the Lord Jesus Christ's case. Over Him, death had no power at all. It is of Him that Paul wrote, *"who only hath immortality"* (1 Tim. 6:16). Who could, without His consent, have laid a hand upon the Prince of Life, the Son of God, and said to Him, "You shall die"? No one could have done that. It was a purely voluntary act for Christ to die at all, not merely to die on the cross. Consequently, this is a telling proof of His love.

There Were No Claims upon Him

Remember, again, that those for whom Christ died had no claims upon Him. I can understand why a mother would lay down her life for her children:

The Limitless Love of Christ

Can a woman forget her sucking child,
that she should not have compassion on
the son of her womb?   *(Isa. 49:15)*

I can understand why the six principal burgesses of Calais put the ropes round their necks and went to Edward the Third to offer to die instead of their fellow citizens. Were they not the leaders of that community? Were they not put into a position of responsibility and honor where, if they were men of truly noble spirit, they would render the necessary sacrifice themselves?

When Queen Eleanor sucked the poison from her husband's wounds, at the risk of her own life, I can see reasons why she did it. I am not suggesting that she was obliged to make such a sacrifice, but I do think that the relationship of a wife accounts for what she did.

Yet, there were no such claims upon our Lord Jesus Christ. The Son of God had no relationship to us until He chose to assume one out of infinite compassion. There was no more relationship between Him and us than between the potter and the clay; and if the clay upon the wheel goes amiss, what does the potter do with it except throw it into a corner? The great Creator could have done the same with us. Instead, He shed His blood in order to make us into vessels of honor, fit for His own use.

How could the Son of God stoop so low as to take our nature upon Himself? He bled and died in that nature, when between us and Him there was a distance infinitely greater than that between an ant and an angel. With no claims upon Him, of His own free will, He yielded Himself to die because of His amazing love for us.

He Was Not Asked to Die

Another extraordinary thing about the love of Christ was that there were no appeals made to Him to die. In the other cases that I have cited, you may remind me that there were no vocal appeals made. The little children in the cradle did not beg their mother to die for them. No, but the very sight of them was enough to plead with their mother. And in the case of the city dying of pestilence, could the surgeon—who believed that he might discover the secret of the evil through a simple examination—could he go through the streets and walk past the doors stamped with the fatal mark and hear the wailing of the widows and the children without feeling pity for them in his heart?

However, man made no appeal to God to die for him. Our father Adam, the representative of us all, did not fall down on his knees in the presence of God and say, "God be merciful to me, a sinner. O God, whom I have offended, provide for me a Savior, and deliver me from Your wrath!" No, not a single prayer came from Adam's lips, not even a confession. There was only a wicked and mean attempt to cast the blame upon God for his disobedience: *"The woman whom thou gavest to be with me, she gave me of the tree, and I did eat"* (Gen. 3:12).

That is all that human nature usually does. It will not admit that it needs a Savior, and it will not confess that it has sinned enough to need an expiatory sacrifice. We did not plead for mercy; we did not ask for an atonement; we did not desire expiation for our sin. Yet Jesus came, unasked, undesired, unsought, to lay down His life for sinners.

No Love in Return

Jesus Christ well knew that, in laying down His life, He would get no love in return from those for whom He died unless He himself created that love. This He has done in the hearts of His own people.

However, in the hearts of others who have been left to themselves, there is no love for

Jesus Christ. Sunday after Sunday, it is my privilege to preach a dying Savior to dying sinners. Yet, of all themes in the world, it seems to make the least impression upon some of my hearers. If I were to talk only of one philanthropist's devotion to helping the prisoners in our jails, many churchgoers would be moved to admiration. In contrast, how little admiration most men have for our sweet Lord! It is an old story, you say, and you have heard it so often that you care little for it.

Now, that mother who died to save her children felt that they loved her. They had often charmed her with their smiles and their cooing while they lay in her arms, and she felt that she could freely give up her life for them. Conversely, Christ knew that He was dying for stony-hearted monsters who, if left to themselves, would utterly reject Him in return for His love. They would not believe in Him. They would trust in their own righteousness rather than in His. They would try to find a way to heaven by sacraments and ceremonies rather than by faith in His sacrifice on the cross.

He Died for Those Who Killed Him

Remember, too, that our Lord died by the hands of men, as well as for the sake of men.

The surgeon at Marseilles did not die by any act of his fellow citizens. The mother did not die at the hands of her children. Curtius, leaping into the gulf, was not forced there by the anger of his fellow countrymen. On the contrary, they died by their own volition, and everyone would have been glad if they had continued to live.

However, it was this that made the death of Christ so sadly unique: He came to die for men who wished to put Him to death. *"Crucify him, crucify him,"* (Luke 23:21) they cried in their mad rage, foaming at the mouth.

"Oh!" say some of you, "but we never said that." No, not then; but perhaps you are saying it now. There are still many who hate the Gospel of Christ, and to hate the Gospel is to hate Christ Himself, for the Gospel is His very essence and heart. Rejecting Christ, choosing your own pleasure, delaying to repent, and living at enmity against Christ are very much the same thing as crying, *"Crucify him."* In the long run, they are the same.

But, you do not see it this way. If you could be quite sure that there is no Christ, no God, no heaven, and no hell, you would be perfectly happy. That is, if it were possible for you to put Christ out of existence, along with everything that has to do with Him, you would.

Well, the very same spirit made the Jews of old
cry, *"Crucify him, crucify him."*

He Became Sin and Shame for Us

Christ's death was also remarkable because, in dying for us, He was taking upon
Himself an awful mass of shame and dishonor,
and also a most intimate connection with sin.
There was nothing shameful about the leap of
Curtius into the chasm. Had I been there to
see him, I would have clapped my hands and
cried, "Well done, Curtius!" Who would not
have said the same? But, when our Lord died,
men thrust out their tongues at Him and
mocked Him. His was indeed a shameful death.

When that mother put her babes up in a
place of safety and threw herself into the raging flood, the angels might have smiled as well
as sorrowed at such a deed of heroism; but
when Jesus hung on the cross to save us, even
God Himself did not smile at Him. Among our
Savior's expiring cries was that agonizing ut-
terance, *"My God, my God, why hast thou forsaken me?"* (Matt. 27:46).

This was because He had, as our Representative, come into contact with human sin,
and so with human shame. The just and holy
Son of God was made a curse for us. As Paul

told us, God *"hath made him to be sin for us, who knew no sin; that we might be made the righteousness of God in him"* (2 Cor. 5:21).

All this helps to manifest to us Christ's amazing love. As the text says, *"Hereby perceive we the love of God, because he laid down his life for us."* Have you and I perceived that love? Do we know it? That is a very simple question, yet I press it upon you.

I think it was Aristotle who said that it is impossible for a person to know that he is loved without feeling some love in return. I think, as a rule, that is true. So, if you really do perceive that Christ loved you so much as to die for you, love for Him will leap up in your heart.

One Sunday night in Exeter Hall, I was reading the hymn that begins, "Jesu, Lover of my soul." There strayed into the hall a man of fashion, a man of the world, careless of all spiritual things. Just then, that line, "Jesu, Lover of my soul," caught his ear. He said to himself, "Does Jesus really love *me*? Is He the Lover of my soul?" That line was the means of generating love in his thoughtless heart, and there and then he surrendered himself to the love of Christ.

Perhaps the same will result by my repeating the story here. I pray that some of you, who have never loved the Lord Jesus Christ before, would now say, "Did He thus love His enemies, thus strangely love them even to the death? Then we, though we have until now been His enemies, can be His enemies no longer. Rather, we will love Him in return for His great love for us."

Christians in Deed

You Christian people who *do* love Him, if you have perceived His love somewhat, try to perceive it still more, so that you may love Him more. If you really love Him, try to show that you do. Notice the rest of the verse from which my text is taken. I did not leave out the latter part because I was afraid of it, but because I did not have time to deal with it as it deserves: *"Hereby perceive we the love of God, because he laid down his life for us: and we ought to lay down our lives for the brethren."*

We ought to prove our love for our God by our love for our fellow men, and especially by our love for our fellow Christians. We ought to prove our love by our actions toward others. I do not know what the love of some professing Christians is worth. I suppose they would know if they put down how much it costs them in a year. I fear that it does not cost some of them nearly as much for their religion as it does for material indulgences. They pay their chimney sweeps better than they pay their ministers. They take care to spend upon themselves in perfect waste a hundred times as much as they spend upon spreading the Gospel, saving the heathen, helping the poor, or rescuing the fallen.

We do not believe in such Christianity as that, and we certainly do not wish to practice it. If we profess to be Christians, let us be Christians in deed, and let us especially show our love for Christ by loving our fellow Christians. If you see any of them in need, aid them to the utmost limit of your power. If they want cheering and comforting, give them good cheer and comfort. If they need financial aid, let them have that, too.

Many Christians have given themselves up to die in order to save the lives of their fellow Christians. In the old days of persecution, there were always some noble souls who tried to hide away the Christians from those who sought their lives. They did so at the risk of their own lives. Also in those times, some of the old people came tottering before the judge, possibly thinking that they had more faith than the younger ones had and would be missed less. If they had more faith, they were more ready to die and let the younger ones live on, until they grew stronger in faith, hope, and love. (See 1 Corinthians 13:13.)

On the other hand, sometimes the young men would gently push back the fathers and say to them, "No, you are old. You should linger here awhile and teach the very young. We young people are strong, so we will go and die for Christ." There were many contentions in the church of God in persecuting times, as to who should first die for Christ. They were all willing to lay down their lives for their fellow Christians.

Where has this self-sacrificing love gone? I would like to see some of it. I would even wear microscopes over my eyes if I thought that I could so discover it. However, I am afraid I cannot. Why, if we loved each other now as Christians loved each other then, we would be the talk of the town. Even men of the world would say, "See how these Christians love one another." Yet, this is only what we ought to do, so let it be what we will do. God help you to do it, for Christ's sake! Amen.

5

Love at Leisure

Mary, which also sat at Jesus' feet,
and heard his word.
—Luke 10:39

Martyrs actively show their love for our Lord and Master by making sacrifices of themselves. Not all of us are martyrs, of course, but once we perceive God's love for us, we will want to love Him more and more through our actions. However, loving God does not always involve active and sacrificial service. No, we can also love our Lord by sitting quietly at His feet, listening to and learning from His every word. This is called love at leisure.

Mary was full of a love for Christ that, at times, could be very active and self-sacrificing. *"It was that Mary which anointed the Lord"* (John 11:2) by pouring a box of precious and fragrant ointment upon His head. She served the Lord after her own fashion, yet she also sat at the Lord's feet, waiting and listening.

Now, because of her servantlike heart, we can look to her not only as a model of active faith, but also as an example of restful faith. The portion of her life occupied in sitting at her Master's feet may instruct and help us. I can safely present her as an example in either case because the Master praised her specifically for anointing Him. He praised her for bringing the box of ointment. (See Luke 7:44–47.) He also praised her as she sat at His feet, saying that she had chosen the good part that would not be taken from her (Luke 10:42). He could not have more conspicuously set His seal of approval on her conduct than He did. If we ever serve the Lord as Mary did, we shall do well.

Those of you who love the Lord as Mary did will find both rest and encouragement in following her example of sitting at the feet of the Lord Jesus Christ. This is the restful side of faith. Consider it well, for I am persuaded that this is the true preparation for the more active service. Contemplation and rest at the Savior's feet will give you the strength that will enable you to anoint His feet and actively serve Him afterwards.

Let us consider, then, Mary sitting at our Savior's feet. We will investigate four points: love at leisure, sitting down; love in lowliness, sitting at Jesus' feet; love listening—she heard His words; and love learning—she held His words close to her heart.

Love at Leisure: Sitting Down

I especially want you to notice the first point, love at leisure. If you have a family to feed and clothe, you know how you are busy all day long—very busy, perhaps. One or both parents are working from early morning until late in the evening. The children have gone to school, and a hundred household things have yet to be done.

However, later in the evening, the meal is over, and there is a warm fire burning. It is pleasant to have the family gathered around the fire, to sit still for a little while to talk, and to indulge in the full meaning of "home." May we never cease to think of the word "home" as the most musical word that ever dropped from mortal lips!

It is in such a setting that love is quiet and still, even careless. Outside it has to watch its words, but inside it is playful, at ease, fearless of all adversaries. Inside it takes its rest. The armor is put off, and the soldier feels the day's battle is done. He is among those that love him, so he no longer stands on his guard.

I do not know what life would be like without some of those sweet leisure moments when love has nothing else to do except to love. Those intervals are like oases in the desert of life, wherein to love is to be happy, and to be loved is to be doubly blessed.

Set Service Aside for Awhile

Christian people ought to have such times. A first step toward loving at leisure is to put aside our service for awhile. Often, those who are busily occupied in the Master's work will overlook the necessity for love to be at leisure. Now, right now, you that work the longest, toil the most, and have to think the hardest can ask the Lord to make this a leisure time between you and Him. You are not called upon to help Martha prepare the banquet. Just sit still now. Sit still and rest at Jesus' feet, and let nothing else occupy you except sitting still and loving and being loved by Him.

Let us try to banish all church cares, too. Holy cares should not always trouble us, yet we often turn our attentions to our service in the church. A preacher, before he goes up to the pulpit, says to himself, "I will try not to think about how I shall preach, or how this part of the sermon may suit one class of my hearers or that part another. I will just be as Lazarus was, of whom it is written, *'Lazarus was one of them that sat at the table with him'*" (John 12:2).

The preacher may often find himself like Martha, overburdened with much serving, if he forgets that he is but a servant of the Master and has only to do His bidding. You might excuse him once or twice, but you should not do so all the time. Whether you are deacon or elder, preacher or hearer, there are times when you must have nothing to do with anything outside of our blessed Lord and your own heart.

As to the Lord's work, we may well take leisure for love because the saving of those souls is His work. It will go on rightly enough. It is good that we are so eager; it would be better if we were even more eager. But for now, we should lay even our eagerness aside, for it is not ours to save; it is His, and He will do it. The Lord will soon allow you to see the concerns of His soul. Christ did not die in vain. The election of the saints is not going to change, and redemption's purpose will not be turned aside. Therefore, rest.

Rid Yourself of Worldly Cares

Can we not get rid of worldly cares? We get enough of them during the six days of the week. Why do we keep them around? We should learn to cast the whole burden of them upon our Lord (1 Pet. 5:7). Let us roll them up and leave them all at the throne of grace. (See Hebrews 4:16.) They will last well enough until tomorrow, and they will undoubtedly plague us enough then, unless we have faith enough to master them. But for now, put them on the shelf. Say, "I will have nothing to do with you now—any one of you. My soul has gone away from you, up to the Savior, to rest and to delight in Him."

Love will claim a time for her own rest. Even though Martha is getting a feast ready for Christ, we will not hear the clatter of dishes or the preparation of the festival. We must just sit there at His feet, look up, and have no eyes except for Him, no ears except for Him, no heart except for Him. It will be love's leisure for the moment.

Our Salvation Is Complete

In truth, we have plenty of reason for resting. We can sit at Jesus' feet because our salvation is complete. He said, *"It is finished"* (John 19:30), and He knew that He had wrought it all. The ransom price has been paid for your soul. Not one drop has been withheld of the blood that is your purchase. The robe of righteousness (Isa. 61:10) is woven from top to bottom; there is not one thread for you to add. It is written, *"Ye are complete in him"* (Col. 2:10). However frail we are, we are still *"perfect in Christ Jesus"* (Col. 1:28), and in spite of all our sin we are still *"accepted in the beloved"* (Eph. 1:6).

If this is true, then love has room for leisure. This thought is like a long couch upon which you may stretch yourself and find that there is space enough for you to take your fullest ease. The restfulness of love is not like the peace of the ungodly, of whom it is said, *"The bed is shorter than that a man may stretch himself upon it"* (Isa. 28:20). Here is perfect rest for you, a couch long enough and broad enough for all your needs.

And, if you should suddenly remember that you still have sin and corruption to overcome in your heart, then be assured that

Christ has put away all your sin. He is *"the end of the law for righteousness to everyone that believeth"* (Rom. 10:4). He has overcome the world on your behalf and said to you, *"Be of good cheer"* (John 16:33).

You must, of course, fight the trickery of the Devil, but your foe is a routed foe. You are battling a broken-headed dragon, and the victory is sure, for your Savior has pledged Himself to it. You may well take your leisure, for the past is blotted out and the future is secure. You are a member of Christ's body, and as such you cannot die. You are a sheep of His pasture, and as such He will never lose you. You are a jewel of His crown, and as such He will never take His eye or His heart from you. Surely, then, you may take your leisure.

Rest in His Mercies

We can also rest at our Master's feet because we have received so much from Him. If your heart longs to love at leisure, be sure to remember that you have many mercies yet to receive, but not as many as you have had already. You have great things yet to learn, but not such great things as you have been taught already.

When you took Christ Jesus to be your Savior, you found more than you will ever find again, even though you find a heaven. Heaven itself is in the loins of Christ, so whoever has Jesus has an eternity of bliss in Him. If God gave Christ to you, all else is small when compared with the Gift you already have. Take your leisure, then, and rejoice in the Lord Himself and in His infinite perfections.

Put Aside Your Worries

Besides, what can the heart do, after all, being so little and so altogether insignificant? If you worry yourself into your grave, what can you accomplish? God did well enough before you were born, and He will do well enough when you are gone. Therefore, do not fret.

I have sometimes heard of ministers who have been quite exhausted by the preparation of a single sermon. I am told, indeed, that one sermon on a Sunday is as much as any man can possibly prepare. It is laborious work to develop a sermon. Then I ask myself, "Did my Lord and Master require His servants to preach such sermons as that? Would they not do more good if they spoke of the simplest truths of the Gospel from their hearts?"

I turn to the Old Testament, and I find that He told His priests to wear white linen, but He also told them never to wear anything that caused sweat (Ezek. 44:18). From this I gather that He did not want His priests in the temple to be sweating and toiling like slaves. He meant that His service should never be wearisome to them, although they threw their strength into it. He is not a taskmaster like Pharaoh, exacting his quota of bricks and then a double quota, giving his servants no straw with which to make them. (See Exodus 5:6–19.) No, but He says,

> *Take my yoke upon you, and learn of me; for I am meek and lowly in heart: and ye shall find rest unto your souls. For my yoke is easy and my burden is light.*
> *(Matt. 11:29–30)*

Therefore, with all the work His people do—and they ought to do it so as to pour their lives on His head like a box of precious ointment—He did not mean to have them stewing and worrying themselves to death. They will do His service much better if they will come often, sit down at His feet, and say, "Now I have nothing to do but to love Him, nothing to do but to receive His love into my soul."

If you will seek after such quiet communion, you will be given power to work—a holy might that will consume you. Take in the strength for the work by first resting at the

Savior's feet. You will have such peace and restfulness, such quiet and calm, that you will be in no hurry from fear or fright. *"He that believeth shall not make haste"* (Isa. 28:16). You will be like the great Eternal who never breaks the leisure in which His supreme mind dwells.

If you cannot keep up leisure to that degree, at least have it on the Sabbath. I invite you, persuade you, and entreat you, beloved Marys and others like you, to do nothing but just enjoy the leisure of love and sit at Jesus' feet.

Love in Its Lowliness

The second thing is love in its lowliness. Love wants to spend her time with Christ: she picks her place, and her place is down at His feet. She does not come to sit at the table with Him, like Lazarus, but she sits down on the ground at His feet.

Do Not Take a Position of Honor

Observe that love in this case does not take the position of honor. She is not a busy housewife, managing affairs, but a lowly worshipper who can only love. Some of us have to be managers for Christ, managing this and managing that, but perhaps love is most at home when she forgets that she has anything to manage. She leaves it to manage itself. Better still, she trusts the Lord to manage it all and just subsides from a manager into a disciple, from a worker into a penitent, from a giver into a receiver, from a somebody—which grace has made her—to a nobody.

Love is glad to be nothing, content to be at His feet, just letting Him be everything while self sinks away. Do not let me simply write about this, but let it be done. Love your Lord now. Let your heart remember Him. Gaze upon His robes of love, all crimsoned with His heart's blood. You can choose to look up to Him either on the cross or on the throne, whichever is easier for you. In any case, say unto Him, "Lord, what am I, and what is my heritage, that You have loved me so?" (See Psalm 8:4.)

Recognize Your Lowly State

Sit near your Lord, but sit at His feet. Let such words as these be upon your lips:

Lord, I am not worthy to be called by Your grace. I am not worthy to be written in Your Book of Life. I am not worthy that You should waste a thought on me, much less that You should shed Your blood for me. I remember what I was when You first dealt with me. I was cold, careless, and hard toward You, but very wanton and eager toward the world, giving my heart away to a thousand lovers and seeking comfort anywhere except in You.

And, when You did come to me, I did not receive You. When You knocked at my door, I did not open to You, though Your head was wet with dew and Your locks with the drops of the night. And, since through Your grace I have admitted You, and You and I have been joined together in a blessed union, yet how unfavorably I have treated You! O my Lord, how little I have done for You! How little I have loved You!

I could faint in Your presence to think that if You examined me and cross-questioned me, I could not answer even one of the thousand questions You might ask me. Your Book accuses me of negligence in reading it. Your throne of grace accuses me of slackness in prayer. The assemblies of Your people accuse me that I have not been enthusiastic in worshipping.

There is nothing in providence, nature, or grace that would not bring some accusation against me. The world itself might blame me for not rebuking it enough, and my very family might charge that I do not bless my household as I should.

If this is your prayer, then you are right, dear brother or sister. Sink; go on sinking; be little; be less; be less still; be still less; be least of all; then be nothing. As you sit at His feet, I hope you have nothing to do but to think of Him, nothing to do but be lowly in His presence, nothing to do but listen to His words and drink in His teaching.

However, there are some of you who do not love Him. It may be that God will lay you low by affliction (Ps. 107:24) in order to bring you to the feet of Jesus. Perhaps He will allow disaster and disappointment to overtake you in the world to win you to Himself. (See Job 33:29–30.) If any of you have had this experience or are passing through it just now, do not trifle with it. While we are in this life, if the Lord comes to us to remind us of our sin, He does it in the greatness of His mercy. Through our trials and testing, we look to Him, and He brings salvation to us.

Look to Him and Praise Him

Lift up your eyes from your lowly place to Him who merits all your praise. Say to Him,

Who are You, that You have thought of
me, that You took me to be Yours even before the earth came into existence, and
then for me left the royalty of heaven for
the poverty of earth? Who are You that
You have gone down to the grave that You
might lift me up and make me to sit with
You at Your right hand? Oh! You have
wrought many wonders for me, and I am
not worthy of the least of Your mercies.
You have given me great and unspeakable
blessings.

If You had only let me be a door
keeper in Your house, I would have been
happy; but You have set me among
princes. If You had given me the crumbs
from Your table, as dogs are fed, I would
have been satisfied; but You have put me
among the children. If You had said that I
might just stand outside the gates of
heaven now and then to hear Your voice
on gala days, it would have been bliss for
me; but now You have promised me that I
will be with You where You are, to behold
Your glory and to partake of it for all
eternity.

Do such thoughts cause you to humble
yourself? I do not know how it is with you, but
the more I think of the Lord's mercies, the
more I sink downward. He has lavished so
much upon us, and so many of us give Him no

return at all. At least, that is how it seems to my heart.

What about you? What are your faith, your love, your liberality, your prayer, your work? Dare you call them anything? Do you imagine that the Lord is pleased with your past? Would He not rather say to you,

> *Thou hast bought me no sweet cane with money, neither hast thou filled me with the fat of thy sacrifices; but thou hast made me to serve with thy sins, thou hast wearied me with thine iniquities.* (Isa. 43:24)

Thus, we sit down again at His feet, and from that place we do not wish to rise. Love's lowliness will be spent in acts of humiliation. We will bow at the feet that were pierced for our redemption.

Love Listening

But now, in the third place, is love listening. Mary sat in the place of humility, but she sat where she could catch each word as it fell, and she was there with that objective. Love wishes to hear all that Christ has to say, and she wishes to hear it close at hand. She wants to hear the very tones in which He speaks and the accents with which He delivers each precept.

She loves to look up and see the eye that has such meaning in it and the countenance that speaks as much as the lips themselves. So, she sits there, and she looks with her eyes toward Him. Then, with her ears and her eyes, she drinks in what He has to say.

Listen to His Words

I want you to do the same. Say in prayer now, *"Speak, LORD, for thy servant heareth"* (1 Sam. 3:9); and then with your ears open, hear what He says by His Word. Perhaps something here has come home to your soul today. Hear it. Hear it well.

It would be almost useless for anyone to try to preach a sermon in the center of the city in midday. If you stood with all that traffic going by and all that rumbling, roaring, and shouting, church bells could sound, and you would hardly hear them. Yet, when it is night and all is still, then you can hear the city clocks strike; then you might hear a man's voice through the streets, even though it was not a very strong one, as he delivered a message to any listeners nearby.

Our Lord often takes advantage of those quiet times when a man has a broken leg and cannot get to work but must be still in the hospital, or when he is unable to get about the house to attend to his ordinary duties but is so helpless that he cannot do anything else but think. Then comes the Lord, and He begins to remind us what we have done in days past, and He talks with us as He never has the opportunity of doing at any other time. The Lord will come to us when the city of our lives has become quiet.

It is far better to find this time ourselves, however, so that the Lord will not need to afflict us in order to get us at His feet. Oftentimes the Good Shepherd, in caring for the sheep, makes us lie down (Ps. 23:2), but He is glad when we come of our own accord, so that we may rest and listen to His Word. What He says to us is for our benefit.

If the Lord is speaking to you, incline your ear, and listen to His voice, however harshly it may seem to sound. You might not want to undergo His scrutiny while you are here on earth, but it will be quite another thing in the next life, if you die unrepentant and unforgiven. Then you may indeed dread the coming of God to bring your sin to remembrance.

Even if He should strip you, be glad to be stripped by Him. If He should wound you and bruise you, willingly give yourself up to be wounded and bruised by Him. Even if He should slay you, rejoice to be slain by Him.

(See Job 13:15.) Remember that He clothes those whom He strips, He heals those whom He wounds, and He makes alive those whom He kills. (See Deuteronomy 32:39.) So, it is a blessed thing to undergo all those terrible operations at the hands of the Most High, for it is in that way that He comes to those whom He means to bless.

Listen to What Is around You

Listen, also, to what He is saying to you by providence. Perhaps a dear child is sick at home, or you have losses in business. It might not seem to you as if these things come from your loving Lord, but perhaps they are the pressure of His hand, drawing you to His side, telling you His secret. Perhaps mercy has come to you in another way. You have prospered; you have been converted; you have had much joy in your family. Well, the Lord's voice is in all that He does to His people, so listen to it. If you listen, you will be obliged to say, "What will I give back to the Lord for His gifts to me?"

Listen to the Still, Small Voice

Listen also to what the Spirit says in your soul. Listen, for it is not until you get your soul quiet that you can hear what the Spirit of God is saying. The clatter of worldliness or pride or some other noise in the soul of man will drown out the still, small voice of the Holy Spirit, to the serious detriment of any disciple. Set aside *all* your cares. As you cast all your cares upon Him (1 Pet. 5:7), sit down at Jesus' feet, and listen. While you listen in that fashion, in lowly spirit at His feet, you are likely to hear Him say some word to you that could change the whole tenor of your life.

I do not know exactly what God will speak, but *"he will speak peace unto his people"* (Ps. 85:8). Sometimes He speaks in such a way that a turbid life becomes clear or a life of perplexity becomes decidedly and distinctly happy. Sometimes when He speaks, a life of weakness becomes a career of strength, or a life that seemed wasted for a while suddenly springs up into eminent usefulness. Keep your ears open. Keep listening, and you will hear what Jesus Christ has to say.

Sit down and listen. Listen as much to Him as to His words, for Christ Himself is the Word and His whole life is a voice. I wish I could put aside my daily routine, sit down for myself, and just look up at Him. He is God over everything, blessed forever, and yet brother to my soul, a partaker of flesh and blood! This fact, that He is incarnate, speaks to me. My soul is comforted, as no words could convey, in the knowledge that God is in human flesh: God took on my nature and became my brother, my helper, my head, my all! My soul could leap out of my body for joy at the incarnation, even if that were the only thing revealed to us.

Listen to What Is Unspoken

Look up again, and see our Lord with His wounds. Mary did not see Him this way, but we now may. See His pierced hands and feet, His scarred side and marred visage, tokens of the ransom price He paid in His pangs and griefs and death. Is it not astounding to see your sin forever blotted out, and blotted out so fully, by such means as this? Why, if there were not an audible word, those wounds would be mouths that speak His love. The most eloquent mouths that ever spoke are the wounds of Christ. Listen! Listen! Every drop of blood says, "Peace." Every wound says, "Pardon, life, eternal life."

Now, look to your Lord again. He is risen from the dead, and His wounds bleed no more. He has gone into His glory, and He sits at the right hand of God the Father. It is well that you cannot literally sit at His feet while He sits in such glory. If you could see Him as He is, I know what would happen to you. It would be what happened to John when he saw Him with His head and His hair white like wool and as white as snow, His eyes as a flame of fire, and His feet as if they burned in a furnace. You would swoon away, as John did. John admitted, *"When I saw him I fell at his feet as dead"* (Rev. 1:14–17).

You cannot literally sit at those feet of glory until you have left this mortal clay, or until it has been made like His glorious body. However, you may do so in faith, and what will His glory say to you? It will say, "This is what you will receive; this is what you will share; this is what you will see forever and ever." He will say to you—even to you who mourn your insignificance and in lowliness sit at His feet— "Beloved, you shall partake of the glory that the Father gave Me, even that which I had with Him before the world was. Soon, when a few more moons have waxed and waned, soon you will be with Me where I am."

Oh, what bliss! Never mind Martha's frowns. Forget her for the moment, and keep sitting at Jesus' feet. She may come in and grumble and say that something is being neglected. Tell her she should not neglect it, then. Right now, your business is not with plates or pots and pans, but to do as your

Master has permitted you to do, namely, to sit at His feet and listen to Him.

Love Learning

My final point here is that love is learning. While Mary sat in the posture of lowliness and listened at Jesus' feet, she was being taught because she was hearing His words as few could hear them. She listened so as to perceive their secret meaning.

Discover His Secret Meaning

A man's voice very near to you sounds somewhat different than that same voice at a distance. You know how much the face can say, what the eyes and the lips can say. Many a deaf man has heard another speak, though he has never heard a sound. He has known the meaning by the very motion of the lips and the expression of the countenance. Likewise, if you get into such close fellowship with Christ as to sit at His feet, you will understand His meaning. When the letter kills others (2 Cor. 3:6), you will see the secret meaning that is hidden within, and you will rejoice.

Mary perceived His meaning, for she was hearing the words so as to drink in their meaning. *"They sat down at thy feet,"* says the old Scripture, *"every one shall receive of thy words"* (Deut. 33:3). In truth, that is a great promise—to receive of His words. Some people hear the words, but do not receive them. Yet, as Mary sat, the words dropped upon her as snowflakes drop into the sea and are absorbed. Each word of Jesus dropped into her soul and became part and parcel of her nature, firing and filling her very being.

Remember His Words

After discovering the meaning of what Christ has said, love treasures up what it has learned. Mary never forgot what she heard that day. It remained with her and seasoned her whole life. After they had been spoken, the words of her Master were with her all the days she was watching and waiting. They kept her watching and waiting, until at last the time was come. It was just before the Savior's death and burial, and she went upstairs where she had put away the choice ointment. She brought it down, and she poured out in adoration the gift that she had hoarded up for Him.

Learn to Love Him Better

As she sat at His feet, Mary resolved to love Him more and more. As she listened and learned, the learning crystallized itself into intense devotion to Christ. Love was learning to love better. Perhaps she had saved up the large sum of money for the ointment little by little, so it was very dear to her. When the time was come, she brought it down and poured it on Him with a joyous liberality and love.

If you wish to learn of Jesus after that fashion, when the time comes, you, too, may do some deed for Christ that will fill your house with sweet perfume. You might even fill the whole earth with the scent, and God Himself will be delighted with the fragrance that you pour out of love upon His Son.

One of the most dreadful things that can ever be said of a man is that he does not love Christ. I would be sorry to include among my friends a man who did not love his mother; more than this, I would not call him a man. His heart is dead to every noble sentiment; and yet, there might be some way to excuse even that. However, not to love Christ, who stooped to bleed for man, is inexcusable! Paul said, *"If any man love not the Lord Jesus Christ, let him be Anathema Maranatha"* (1 Cor. 16:22), which means "cursed at the coming."

Sometimes when I think of my Lord, and my heart is bursting with admiration for His self-denying love, I could almost curse those who do not love Him. Instead, however, I ask His blessing for them, and I say, *"Father, forgive them; for they know not what they do."* (Luke 23:34).

Learn to love Him. Sit at His feet and listen to His words. Treasure them and meditate upon them, and you will find the restful side of faith.

May God's blessing rest on these words. Amen.

6

Unparalleled Lovingkindnesses

Lord, where are thy former lovingkindnesses, which thou swarest unto David in thy truth?
—Psalm 89:49

Love at its leisure, sitting at the Savior's feet, finds a very restful faith. When we spend time listening to the words of our Lord, our hearts become satisfied, and we have no doubt about the surety of our salvation. We know we have a covenant with God that is everlasting, sealed by the blood of Christ, and we know that our lives with Him become filled with His lovingkindness. Only when we forget to spend that time with the Lord, or when sin stands between us and His presence, do we fail to see the bountiful mercies with which He has blessed us.

The Lord had also made an everlasting covenant with David. Though it was ordered in all things and it was sure, that covenant was not intended to preserve David from trouble. When the eighty-ninth psalm was written, David had been brought very low. His crown had been cast down to the ground, his enemies had rejoiced over him, and he had become a reproach to his neighbors. Then, his thoughts flew back to the happier days of the past and the covenant that the Lord had made with him. Either David himself, or Ethan writing on his behalf, inquired, *"Lord, where are thy former lovingkindnesses, which thou swarest unto David in thy truth?"*

Applying this passage to the people of God, I will touch upon four points: first, that we have received mercies in the past; secondly, that we are not always conscious of the flow of God's mercy toward us; thirdly, that there are reasons why we are not always conscious of it; and finally, that the divine covenant remains firm and steadfast under all changing circumstances.

Abundant Mercies

So I remark, first, that we have received many mercies in the past. Is that too common a matter for you to think and talk about? If you know it so well, why do you forget it so often? The mercies of God wake us every morning, so that we are as used to them as we are to the sunlight, yet some of us take them for granted. They follow us through the night, and we get as accustomed to them as we do to our beds, yet some of us might even think less of them than we do of our beds.

We have providential mercies every moment of the day and every day of our lives. We can never tell the number of them, for they are more than the sands upon the seashore. In this chapter, we will look into the spiritual mercies with which God has enriched us—the blessings of the upper springs. I will help you to recall them by referring to the list in Psalm 103:

Bless the LORD, O my soul, and forget not all his benefits: who forgiveth all thine iniquities; who healeth all thy diseases; who redeemeth thy life from destruction; who crowneth thee with lovingkindness and tender mercies; who satisfieth thy mouth with good things; so that thy youth is renewed like the eagle's. (Ps. 103:2–5)

Forgiven of Sin

In the third verse, we find: *"who forgiveth all thine iniquities."* If we are truly the children of God, we should constantly remember that we are pardoned souls. There was a time when we were not. What would we not have given then to know what we know now? At that time, our iniquities pressed upon us as a burden that we could not bear, the stings of conscience gave us no rest, and the terrors of hell had their hold upon us.

When I was under conviction of sin, I felt that I would willingly have given my eyes, my hands, my all, just to be able to say, "I am a forgiven soul." Now that we are pardoned, let us not forget the Lord's lovingkindness in forgiving all our iniquities. If you can forget this, I wonder whether your iniquities have, in fact, ever been forgiven. The pardon of sin is so great a mercy that the song it evokes from the heart must last forever.

Healed of Diseases

The next mercy in the psalmist's list is: *"who healeth all thy diseases"* (v. 3). Try to remember what the Lord has done for you in this respect. Once, pride possessed you like a burning fever and long prevented you from submitting to God's simple plan of salvation. Now, you have been cured of that terrible malady, and you are sitting humbly at the feet of Jesus, rejoicing in being saved by grace.

Perhaps you were once like the Gadarene demoniac. (See Mark 5:1–8.) The chains of morality could not bind you, and the fetters of human law could not restrain you. You cut and wounded yourself, and you were a terror to others. Now, you are so completely healed by God's power that there is not even a scar left to show where you were wounded. Will you not praise the Lord for this unspeakable mercy? What would you not have given for it when your many diseases held you in their cruel grip? Do not cease to praise Jehovah Rapha, *"the LORD that healeth thee"* (Exod. 15:26).

Secured from Destruction

The next mercy also demands a song of grateful praise: *"who redeemeth thy life from destruction"* (v. 4). You have been saved from going down into the pit; the ransom price has been paid for you; and you have been redeemed, not with silver and gold, *"but with the precious blood of Christ, as of a lamb without blemish and without spot"* (1 Pet. 1:19). Remember that there is no wrath against you in the heart of God now, for His righteous anger on account of your sin was all poured out upon the head of His Son, your Surety and Substitute. The Devil has no claim upon you now, for you have been completely redeemed by Christ.

How can you forget to praise Him who has done such great things for you? At one time, what would you not have given for half a hope that you were a redeemed soul? Do you remember when your knees were thoroughly sore from praying so long and your voice was hoarse from crying unto God? You would gladly have bartered the light of day, the comforts of life, and the joys of friendship for the assurance of your redemption. Well, since you have now obtained that priceless boon, do not forget to praise the Lord for all His lovingkindness toward you.

Made Heirs of the Kingdom

The next clause in the fourth verse is: *"who crowneth thee with lovingkindness and tender mercies."* Recollect, again, what the Lord has done for you. Not content with saving you from hell, He has adopted you into His own family, made you a son or a daughter of the King of Kings, and set a royal crown upon your head—a crown of *"lovingkindness and tender mercies."* You are made *"heirs of God, and joint-heirs with Christ"* (Rom. 8:17).

What can parallel this lovingkindness? Is this not, indeed, the tender mercy of our God toward you? Can you ever forget such lovingkindness and tender mercy? There have been times in our personal histories and in our experiences when that ancient prophecy has been graciously fulfilled:

> *Ye shall go out with joy, and be led forth with peace: the mountains and the hills shall break forth before you into singing, and all the trees of the field shall clap their hands.* (Isa. 55:12)

So, as we remember the former lovingkindnesses of the Lord, let us rejoice that He still crowns us with His lovingkindness and tender mercies even today.

Our Hearts Are Satisfied

We must not forget the next verse: *"who satisfieth thy mouth with good things; so that thy youth is renewed like the eagle's"* (v. 5). If we are in Christ Jesus, we have all that we want and are perfectly satisfied. We do not want a better Savior, we do not want a better hope, we do not want a better Bible or a better promise. We do want more faith, but we do not want a better foundation of faith. We do desire to have more love for our Lord, but we do not desire a better object for our love.

We desire to dive deeper and ever deeper, but only in the fathomless sea of Jesus' love. Others are roaming here and there, vainly seeking satisfaction, but our mouths are so filled with good things that we are satisfied. We asked, and the Lord gave. We prayed for pardon, and the Lord fully forgave us for Jesus' sake. We have received so much mercy from Him that our souls are satisfied and soar above as on eagles' wings. We can leave all worldly cares, sorrows, and doubts far below us amid the earthborn clouds; we have ascended high above them by God's grace.

Our Perception of Present Mercies

Now, having thus briefly recalled the Lord's former lovingkindnesses, I have to remind you, in the second place, that we are not always conscious of the flow of the Lord's mercies toward us.

The psalmist asked, *"Lord, where are thy former lovingkindnesses?"* Well, where are they? Why, they are where they used to be, though we do not always realize it. The Lord's mercies have not changed, but our perception of them is not always as vivid as it ought to be. Let us again consider each of the mercies in Psalm 103 in relation to this concept.

We Doubt Our Forgiveness

"Who forgiveth all thine iniquities." There are times when a Christian fears whether his sins are really forgiven. He is saved, yet he doubts whether he is saved or not. All his past sins seem to rise up before him, and plaguing unbelief whispers, "Can it be possible that all those sins have been put away? Have all those mountains of iniquity been cast into the red sea of the Savior's atoning blood?"

Many young believers who judge themselves too much by their feelings are apt to imagine that they have been deceived and that they are still under condemnation. If this is your thinking, let me assure you that there are times when the very best of the saints have to cry out in the bitterness of their souls, *"Lord, where are thy former lovingkindnesses?"*

The believer in Christ is always justified so far as the law of God is concerned, but he does not always hear the proclamation of pardon in the court of his conscience. God's sun is always shining, but there are clouds that obscure its beams. Yet, it is hidden only for a while. It is the same with the lovingkindness of the Lord in regard to the forgiveness of sin. Whether we realize it or not, the forgiveness that has once been bestowed upon us will never be withdrawn from us for all eternity.

We Doubt Our Healing

It is the same with the next mercy: *"who healeth all thy diseases."* Some of us know that our Lord, the Great Physician, has healed our soul maladies, yet at times unbelief and other evil diseases cause us pain and agony of spirit. When the fountains of the great deep are broken up (Gen. 7:11), we long to be like Noah, floating in the ark of our faith above the awful sea of our depravity, which threatens to drown every spiritual comfort and cover every hope.

If I were to look within my own heart for comfort and hope, I would often be in despair. However, when I look away to my Lord alone, I realize what He has done and is still doing for me, for He still heals all my diseases. My faith is strengthened the more I focus on Him.

If you cannot see yourself growing in grace as you would like to, do not be surprised. When a farmer goes to look at his root crops, he is not so much concerned with the appearance of the part above ground as with the part that is out of sight.

Likewise, a Christian does much of his growing underground, as it were—growing in grace, knowledge, love, and humility. Of course, he might not have many virtues and graces that are visible to other people, or even to himself. Sanctification is wrought in the saints according to the will of God, but it is a secret work. In due time, belief will replace doubt, and the fruit of it will be manifest, even as the farmer at the proper season digs up his roots and rejoices that his labor has not been expended upon them in vain.

We Doubt Our Redemption

Notice, too, the next mercy: *"who redeemeth thy life from destruction."* Mark that those who are once redeemed are always redeemed. The price of their redemption was paid upon Calvary, and that great transaction can never be reversed. I dare to put it very strongly, and to say that they were as fully redeemed when they were dead in trespasses and sins as they will be when they stand before the eternal throne. They were not then conscious of their redemption, but their unawareness did not alter the fact of their redemption.

So it is with the believer. There are dark days and cloudy days in his experience, but he is just as truly saved in the dark and cloudy day as when the sun is shining brightly and the clouds have all been blown away.

In the old days of slavery, when a slave's freedom had been purchased, there may have been times when he had little to eat or when he had many aches and pains, but such things did not affect the fact that he was a free man. Suppose someone had said to him, "My poor fellow, you have nothing in the cupboard, you are very sick and ill; therefore, you are still a slave."

He would have replied, "That is not good reasoning. I know that I was redeemed, for I saw the price that was paid for my ransom. I have my free papers, and I shall never again be a slave."

So it is with Christians. The Son of God has made them free by giving Himself as a ransom for them, so they are *"free indeed"* (John 8:36). Their redemption does not depend upon their realization of it, but upon their Redeemer, who has made it effective for them.

We Forget the Lord's Mercies

The same principle applies to the next mercy: *"who crowneth you with lovingkindness and tender mercies."* There once was a lesson that one Methodist tried to teach another. As he heard over and over again the story of his brother's trials and troubles, he was grieved, for he heard nothing about the multitudes of mercies with which he was continually being crowned.

So one day he said to him, "My brother, I wish you would change your residence. You do not live in the right part of the town."

"How is that?" inquired the other.

"Why, you live where I used to live, on Murmuring Street. It is very dark and narrow, the chimneys always smoke, the lamps never burn brightly there, and all sorts of diseases abound. I grew tired of living on Murmuring Street, so I took a new house on Contentment Street. It is a fine, wide, open street where the breezes of heaven can freely blow, so the people who dwell there are healthy and happy.

"Remarkably, the houses on the street, though they are all of different sizes, are just the right size for the people who live in them. The apostle Paul used to live on that street, for he said, *'I have learned, in whatsoever state I am, therewith to be content'* (Phil. 4:11). So I would advise you, my brother, to move to Contentment Street as soon as you can." That was very good advice, and we may pass it on to any murmurers or grumblers we might know.

Consider how the Lord is still crowning you with lovingkindness and tender mercies. You might not be strong, but then you do not have that acute pain you used to have. You might be growing old, but that only means that you are getting so much nearer to heaven. You might have fewer friends than you once had, but those who are left are true friends. In all the circumstances of your life, you see that you are still crowned with lovingkindness and tender mercies.

We Forget Our Satisfaction

So it is with the last mercy in the list: *"who satisfieth thy mouth with good things."* I will venture to say that a Christian who is not satisfied with the good things from God does not have one *real* want. If he has any other want, or thinks he has, it is better for him not to have that want supplied.

If we want the pleasures of sin, God demonstrates His mercy by not giving them to us, for the supply of these would be our souls' damnation. If we could gather any comfort through following what is evil, the Lord shows His mercy by not allowing that comfort to be our portion. Besides, what could we possibly want, having Christ?

Why Do We Forget His Mercies?

Now, thirdly, why are we not always conscious of the flow of mercy toward us? There are several reasons for this. The first is that sin prevents us.

Sin Prevents Us

Sometimes we miss our former comforts as the result of sin. Sin indulged is a definite barrier to happiness. No one can enjoy communion with Christ while turning aside to crooked ways. How could you sit at the Lord's feet and listen to His words in the morning while you are indulging in sin at night? The more inconsistent a believer is with his faith, the more unhappy he will be. In this case, it will be no surprise if he has to cry, *"Lord, where are thy former lovingkindnesses?"*

We must always distinguish between the punishment that Christ endured for His people's sin and the fatherly chastisement that God visits upon our wrongdoing. Though He will not condemn us as a Judge, He will chastise us as a Father, and no one can expect to enjoy the lovingkindness of the Lord while enduring the strokes of His rod.

We Neglect the Means of Grace

We may also lose a comfortable sense of God's mercy through neglecting to use the means of grace. Abandon the regular reading of your Bible, and you will be like the man who misses his meals; he grows weak and languid. Neglect private prayer, and then see whether you will not have to cry with Job,

Oh that I were as in months past, as in the days when God preserved me; when his candle shined upon my head, and when by his light I walked through darkness!
(Job 29:2–3)

Stay away from the prayer meeting, and then, if your soul is not deeply troubled, or if your heart is not sad, it ought to be. If a man will not come and stand near the fire, is it surprising that he cries that he cannot get warm? The neglect of the means of grace causes many to inquire, *"Lord, where are thy former lovingkindnesses?"*

Idol Worship Prevents Us

The same result follows when an idol is set up in the heart. As long as we worship the Lord alone, the temples of our hearts will be filled with His glory; but if we set an idol upon His throne, we will soon hear the rushing of wings and the divine voice saying, *"Let us go hence"* (John 14:31). God and mammon cannot abide in the same house (Matt. 6:24). You serve a jealous God (Exod. 34:14), so be very careful not to provoke Him to jealousy. Every idol must be cast down, and the Lord must be before all things in our worship, or His comfortable presence cannot be enjoyed.

Our Hearts Grow Spiritually Cold

Coldness of heart toward God is another cause of the loss of enjoyment of His favor. If the heart is warm and vigorous, the pulsations throughout the entire body will be kept strong and healthy. When the heart grows spiritually cold, however, the whole being soon gets out of order, the blood is chilled in the veins, and all the powers are dulled and paralyzed.

Be sure, then, to maintain the warmth of holy affection that you showed when first you knew the Lord. Maintain your love by the Holy Spirit, or else you will soon have to cry, *"Lord, where are thy former lovingkindnesses?"* Live near to God, and this will not often be your cry; but if you backslide from Him, this will soon be your sorrowful enquiry. If you have to mourn an absent God, seek to know why He has withdrawn Himself from you, and repent of the sin that has separated you from Him.

The Covenant Is Steadfast

While we may forget and doubt the mercies of our Lord, He does not falter or fail us. This is the fourth point I want to make in regard to our text. Let us remember that the divine covenant remains firm and steadfast under all changing circumstances. The covenant made with David was established by the oath of God. Paul, writing to the Hebrews, said,

> *Wherein God, willing more abundantly to show unto the heirs of promise the immutability of his counsel, confirmed it by an oath; that by two immutable things, in which it was impossible for God to lie, we might have a strong consolation, who have fled for refuge to lay hold upon the hope set before us.* (Heb. 6:17–18)

Assured That We Are Chosen

For our consolation, let us remember, first, that the parties to the covenant are always the same. God does not have one set of chosen ones today and another set tomorrow. In the Lamb's Book of Life, names are neither erased nor replaced. No, that is not how the Lord deals with His elect. He does not love them one day and hate them the next. Oh, no!

> Whom once he loves, he never leaves,
> But loves them to the end.

Sealed by the Blood of Christ

Next, the seal of the covenant is always the same. It is sealed with the precious blood of

Jesus. His one great sacrifice on Calvary made the covenant forever sure.

> 'Tis signed, and sealed, and ratified,
> In all things ordered well.

We do not seal the covenant; Christ Himself has done that. His blood makes the covenant sure to everyone for whom He stood as Surety and Substitute. This is our consolation, even when we have no present enjoyment of the blessings secured by the covenant.

Even the sealing of the Spirit is not the seal of the covenant. The sealing of the Spirit is the certain evidence of our interest in the covenant. It is like a seal to our copy of the covenant. However, the great deed itself is sealed with the blood of Jesus. It is safely preserved in the archives of heaven where no one can mutilate or steal or destroy it.

Never to Become Void

Further, the efficacy of the covenant is always the same. It is not like human covenants, which may or may not be fulfilled, or which may become void through a lapse of time. No, this covenant is eternal, covering past, present, and future. It will be fulfilled to the last jot and tittle, for He who swore unto

David will certainly perform all that He has promised to His chosen people (1 Kings 8:56).

> The voice that rolls the stars along
> Speaks all the promises.

When God said, *"Let there be light,"* there was light (Gen. 1:3). Likewise, when that same God says, "Let there be light in that dark soul," light at once enters, and the heart is divinely illuminated. Thus it has come to pass that we, who were once in darkness, are now light in the Lord. Paul admonished us, *"Walk as children of light"* (Eph. 5:8).

The efficacy of the covenant does not depend upon us, either; if it did, it would be a poor, feeble, fickle thing that would fail us just when we need it most. There would be no hope of our ever getting to heaven if we had to depend upon our own efforts, our own merits, or anything of our own. You might recall how, in the first chapter, we discussed what Christ's love has done for us. One of the benefits of His love is that He has become our Representative before the Father. Our comfort arises from the fact that the covenant is made on our behalf by our great Representative, who will Himself see that every guarantee in the covenant is fulfilled in due season.

A glorious chariot of salvation rolls along somewhere, in which all believers are riding to heaven. Neither death nor hell can stop it. All the fears of the people in it will not affect their eternal safety, and not one of these believers will be found missing on the day when the redeemed are called to glory. Be of good courage, believer, for you are saved in the Lord with an everlasting salvation. Even though you mourn the loss of the Lord's former lovingkindnesses, search your heart to see how far that loss has been caused by your own sin. Then, return to the Lord with all your heart (Deut. 30:2), and He will renew to you His former favors and give you new mercies of which you have not even dreamed.

As for those who have no former lovingkindnesses of the Lord to which you can look back, I pray that this may be the beginning of better days for you. Think of the mercies that the Lord has bestowed upon others, and cry unto Him, "Lord, do to me as You have done to them. Adopt me also into Your family as Your son or Your daughter, and let me share in all the blessings that You give to Your children!"

Remember that it is by simple and sincere faith in the crucified Christ of Calvary that sinners are eternally saved. It is by His blood that we, who were once afar off, are now brought near (Eph. 2:13). Whoever believes in Him will not be ashamed or confounded (Isa. 54:4). Therefore, *"believe on the Lord Jesus Christ, and thou shalt be saved"* (Acts 16:31), and God will be glorified. May it be so, for Jesus' sake! Amen.